Beholding Christ...
The Son of God

A Study of John 1 - 5

From the Bible-teaching Ministry of

Charles R. Swindoll

Insight for Living

Charles R. Swindoll graduated in 1963 from Dallas Theological Seminary, where he now serves as the school's fourth president, helping to prepare a new generation of men and women for the ministry. Chuck has served in pastorates in three states: Massachusetts, Texas, and California, including almost twenty-three years at the First Evangelical Free Church in Fullerton, California. He is currently senior pastor of Stonebriar Community Church in Frisco, Texas, north of Dallas. His sermon messages have been aired over radio since 1979 as the *Insight for Living* broadcast. A best-selling author, he has written numerous books and booklets on many subjects.

Editor in Chief:
Cynthia Swindoll
Coauthor of Text:
Ken Gire
Author of Living Insights, Senior Editor, and Assistant Writer:
Wendy Peterson
Editors:
Christina Grimstad
Karla Lenderink
Copy Editor:
Marco Salazar

Rights and Permissions:
The Meredith Agency
Graphic System Administrator:
Bob Haskins
Director, Communications Division:
John Norton
Print Production Manager:
Don Bernstein
Project Coordinator:
Jennifer Hubbard
Printer:
Sinclair Printing Company

Unless otherwise identified, all Scripture references are from the New American Standard Bible, copyright © The Lockman Foundation 1960, 1962, 1963, 1968, 1971, 1972, 1973, 1975, 1977. Used by permission. Scripture taken from the Holy Bible, New International Version, Copyright © 1973, 1978, 1984 International Bible Society, used by permission of Zondervan Bible Publishers [NIV]. The other translation cited is *The New Testament in Modern English* by J. B. Phillips (PHILLIPS).

Based on the outlines, charts and transcripts of Charles R. Swindoll's sermons, the study guide titled *Exalting Christ . . . The Son of God* was renamed in 2000 to *Beholding Christ . . . The Son of God* and the text was revised by Wendy Peterson, senior editor and assistant writer in the Educational Ministries Department of Insight for Living:

Copyright © 2000 by Insight for Living

Guide titled *Exalting Christ . . . The Son of God* coauthored by Ken Gire:
Copyright © 1987 by Charles R. Swindoll, Inc.
Outlines published by New Standard for Living and Insight for Living titled *The Gospel of John:*
Copyright © 1975, 1976 by Charles R. Swindoll, Inc.
Original outlines, charts, and transcripts for series titled *The Gospel of John:*
Copyright © 1975, 1976 by Charles R. Swindoll, Inc.

An effort has been made to locate sources and obtain permission where necessary for the quotations used in this book. In the event of any unintentional omission, a modification will gladly be incorporated in future printings.

ISBN 1-57972-328-4
Cover design by Michael Standlee Design
Cover image © Charles Mauzy/Panoramic Images, Chicago. All rights reserved.
Printed in the United States of America

Contents

Introduction

Jesus Christ is God!

These four words state the theme of John's Gospel. They also convey the underlying message of his first five chapters. His hope is to convince his readers of the undiminished deity of the Son of God. To miss that fact is to miss the message of this fourth book of the New Testament.

These studies are designed to take us back to the first century . . . to clear away all the debris of traditional opinions and personal feelings so that we are able to examine the evidence. When we do, we shall realize that Jesus of Nazareth was, in fact, truly God.

May our Lord use these studies to convince you of His lordship, His majesty, His authority. And as He does, may we behold Him anew!

Chuck Swindoll

Chuck Swindoll

Putting Truth
Into Action

Knowledge apart from application falls short of God's desire for His children. He wants us to apply what we learn so that we will change and grow. This study guide was prepared with these goals in mind. As you go through the following pages, we hope your desire to discover biblical truth will grow as your understanding of God's Word increases, and that you will be encouraged to apply what you've learned.

To assist you in your study, we've included a section called ☀ **Living Insights** at the end of each lesson. These exercises will challenge you to study further and to think of specific ways to put your discoveries into action.

On occasion a lesson is followed by a ✎**Digging Deeper** section, which gives you additional information and resources to probe further into some issues raised in that lesson.

There are many ways to use this guide—in personal devotions, group studies, discussions with friends and family, and Sunday school classes. And, of course, it's an ideal study aid when you're listening to its corresponding *Insight for Living* radio series.

To benefit most from this study guide, we would encourage you to consider it a spiritual journal. That's why we've included space in the **Living Insights** for recording your thoughts and discoveries. We hope you'll return to those sections often for review and encouragement as you continue to grow in your walk with Christ.

Insight for Living

Beholding Christ...
The Son of God

A STUDY OF JOHN 1-5

JOHN

Stage	Deity "The Word was God." (1:1) CHAPTER 1:1–13	God-Man "The Word became flesh." (1:14) *Miraculous signs:* Water into wine (2) Heals official's son (4) CHAPTERS 1:14–4:54	Ministry *Miraculous signs:* Heals invalid at Bethesda (5) Feeds 5,000 (6) Walks on water (6) Heals blind man (9) Raises Lazarus (11) CHAPTERS 5–12	Discourse *Private talks:* Servanthood (13) Heaven (14) Abiding (15) Promises (16) Prayer (17) CHAPTERS 13–17	Trials and Death CHAPTERS 18–19	Empty Tomb *Private talks:* Appearances (20) CHAPTER 20	Assurance *Private talks:* Future (21) CHAPTER 21
	Prologue	Acceptance	Conflict	Preparation	Crucifixion	Triumph	EPILOGUE
Audience	Public message			CHANGE	Private message		
Time	Three years				Several days		
Jesus' Seven "I Am" Statements	• "I am the bread of life." (6:35) • "I am the Light of the world." (8:12) • "I am the door." (10:9) • "I am the good shepherd." (10:11)			• "I am the resurrection and the life." (11:25) • "I am the way, and the truth, and the life." (14:6) • "I am the true vine." (15:1)			
Main Theme and Key Verse	"These have been written so that you may believe that Jesus is the Christ, the Son of God; and that believing you may have life in His name." (20:31)						

Chapter 1

"That You May Believe"

Survey of John

Before we cross the threshold of John's Gospel, we are compelled to take off our shoes, for every page is ablaze with deity. More than with almost any other book, we realize that here we are standing on holy ground. As William Barclay writes:

> For many Christian people the Gospel according to *St. John* is the most precious book in the New Testament. It is the book on which above all they feed their minds and nourish their hearts, and in which they rest their souls. Very often on stained glass windows and the like the gospel writers are represented in symbol by the figures of the four beasts whom the writer of the *Revelation* saw around the throne (*Revelation 4:7*). . . . The *eagle* stands for *John,* because it alone of all living creatures can look straight into the sun and not be dazzled, and John has the most penetrating gaze of all the New Testament writers into the eternal mysteries and the eternal truths and the very mind of God. Many people find themselves closer to God and to Jesus Christ in *John* than in any other book in the world.[1]

I. Background of John's Gospel

John writes with a simple, straightforward style. Seldom will you find a word over three syllables; most are one or two—"In the beginning was the Word, and the Word was with God, and the Word was God" (John 1:1). Simple . . . straightforward . . . yet sublime. John is also a writer fond of contrasts. Light and dark. Life and death. Spirit and flesh. A story may jump from sadness to ecstasy, from stormy conflict to the sweetest calm, from a crisis of doubt to concrete assurance. Another aspect of John's style is that he does not use a running video camera to record the life of

---

1. William Barclay, *The Gospel of John,* rev. ed., The Daily Study Bible Series (Philadelphia, Pa.: Westminster Press, 1975), vol. 1, p. 1.

Jesus. Rather, he uses a more selective snapshot approach. Consequently, John reads more like a thematic scrapbook of Christ's life than a meticulously chronicled documentary.

A. Why are there four Gospels? Why not one definitive biography of Christ rather than four separate accounts? Because a picture is more complete when taken from several different angles. Take sports, for example. The player, the coach, the referee, the fans, and the television cameras all look at a play from different angles. In order to get the fullest possible picture of the play, all angles have to be taken into consideration. Or take another example. The biography of a famous man is not really complete unless we have accounts from all perspectives —from his parents, mate, children, and so forth. Each would see things from a different viewpoint and thus give us a little different slant on his life. The parents would see him as son; the wife, as sweetheart; the children, as Daddy. Similarly, each Gospel writer looks at Jesus from his own distinct angle.[2]

1. Matthew. Matthew, writing to the Jews, was interested in establishing the regal rights of Jesus as King of the Jews. In doing so, he traced the genealogy of Jesus back to David and Abraham. He set forth Christ as the Redeemer-King of Israel, the Messiah promised to the forefathers. The inscription "Behold, your king" (Zech. 9:9) could be written over Matthew's Gospel, summarizing his view of Jesus.

2. Mark. Mark, writing to the Romans, was interested in capturing those shots of Jesus that showed Him as a man of action. Consequently, we have no genealogy in Mark's Gospel; he goes straight to the story and to the interests of his Gentile audience. Mark also revealed Jesus as the suffering Servant, providing a model of discipleship for the persecuted Christians in Rome. Over Mark's Gospel, then, the inscription might read "Behold, My Servant" (Isa. 42:1; see also Zech. 3:8).

3. Luke. Luke was writing to all Christians and the entire Gentile world, focusing on Jesus' humanity. So Luke traced Christ's genealogy all the way back to Adam. Throughout his account, Luke pictured the Son of Man as the Redeemer of the whole human race, as One who

---

2. Helpful books on reconciling the different Gospel accounts are: *A Harmony of the Gospels,* by Robert L. Thomas and Stanley N. Gundry (Chicago, Ill.: Moody Press, 1979); *A Guide to the Gospels,* by W. Graham Scroggie (Old Tappan, N.J.: Fleming H. Revell Co., 1967); *The Words and Works of Jesus Christ: A Study of the Life of Christ,* by J. Dwight Pentecost (Grand Rapids, Mich.: Zondervan Publishing House, 1981).

was willing to save people of every nation. Over his Gospel we might inscribe "Behold, a man" (Zech. 6:12).

4. **John.** John wrote to a timeless, universal audience. More than the other writers, he stressed the deity of Christ and His unique relationship with the Father. Over his Gospel the words "Behold, your God" (Isa. 35:4) could be written in letters of gold.

Ecce Homo

Stop here and take a few minutes to "behold" Jesus.[3] Look at Him from every angle. He is the true King. He is the humble, suffering Servant. He is the quintessential man—all that humanity was created to be. And He is God. Jesus Christ never changes. He is the same yesterday, today, and forever (Heb. 13:8).

Yet how we need Him at a given moment does change. There are times we need to realize that He is King and we are the subjects of His kingdom—times when we need Him to rule firmly and decisively in our lives. In other moments, however, we need Him to wash our feet and teach us, by example, how we are to serve others. Sometimes we need to realize that He was once one of us, that He hungered and hurt, and that He sympathizes with our weaknesses. And there are times in our lives when we need to see Him as God, Creator and Sustainer of the universe, who is in control of our circumstances.

Hold Him up to the light. See every facet of His being sparkle. He is without flaw. Truly, a beautiful Savior!

B. **Why do we have John's Gospel?** John's Gospel differs significantly from the other three.[4] No account of Jesus' birth, baptism, or temptation is given. John tells nothing of the Last Supper, Gethsemane, or the Ascension. No word of the healing

---

3. *Ecce homo* is Latin for "Behold, the Man!" taken from the Vulgate version of Pilate's words when he presented Jesus to the people before the Crucifixion (John 19:5).

4. The accounts of Matthew, Mark, and Luke are commonly referred to as the *synoptic* Gospels, from the Greek word *synoptikos*, meaning "seeing together." To examine the differences between the synoptic accounts and John, see Richard T. France, "Reading the Gospels," in the *New Bible Commentary: 21st Century Edition,* 4th ed., ed. D. A. Carson, R. T. France, J. A. Motyer, and G. J. Wenham (Downers Grove, Ill.: InterVarsity Press, 1994), pp. 896–903.

of any people possessed by devils or evil spirits is found in this Gospel. And, most surprisingly, it documents none of Jesus' parables. However, it does contain much that the others omit. John alone tells us of the wedding feast at Cana (2:1–11); of Nicodemus (3:1–22); of the woman at the well (chap. 4); of the raising of Lazarus (chap. 11); of Jesus washing the disciples' feet (13:1–17); of the teaching about the Holy Spirit as the divine Comforter in the Upper Room Discourse (chaps. 13:31–17:26). Also unique to John are the vignettes of Thomas (11:16; 14:5; 20:24–29), Andrew (1:40–41; 6:8–9; 12:22), and Philip (6:5–7; 14:8–9). But beyond filling in missing snapshots to the scrapbook, John shows Jesus in the full light of His deity more than any of the other writers.

II. Overview of John's Gospel

Traditionally, the author of the Fourth Gospel has been almost unanimously viewed as John, the son of Zebedee and brother of James (Mark 1:19). Prior to becoming a disciple, he was in the fishing business with his brother and Peter (Luke 5:10). Along with Peter and James, he was part of the inner circle of disciples who were allowed to accompany Jesus on certain great occasions (Mark 5:37; 9:2; 14:33). Throughout the Gospel of John he is distinguished as the closest person to Christ, the disciple whom Jesus loved (John 13:23; 19:26; 20:2).[5]

A. What is John's motive? John's purpose for writing his Gospel is explicitly stated in chapter 20.

> Many other signs therefore Jesus also performed in the presence of the disciples, which are not written in this book; but these have been written *that you may believe that Jesus is the Christ*, the Son of God; and that believing you may have life in His name. (vv. 30–31, emphasis added)

At the end of his Gospel, John adds that if everything Jesus did were written down, "even the world itself would not contain the books which were written" (21:25). John, then, had to be selective in what he recorded from the life of Christ. He chose and structured his material in such a way that the narrative would irrefutably reveal the truth that Jesus was indeed the Son of God (see 1:34, 49; 6:69; 10:36; 11:4, 27; 20:28, 31). Having

---

5. The author of the Fourth Gospel is to be distinguished from John the Baptist (mentioned in John 1:6–8), who was not only related to Jesus (Luke 1:36) but also the forerunner to His ministry (Luke 1:13–17; Matt. 3). For an exhaustive discussion of the authorship of the Fourth Gospel, consult *The Gospel of John*, by William Hendriksen (Grand Rapids, Mich.: Baker Book House, 1953), pp. 3–31.

led his readers to the Son, John would have them drink the living water that Jesus offers to all through faith (4:14). *Believe* is one of John's favorite words, used in various forms (*believe, believed, believes—pisteuo*, in Greek) a total of ninety-eight times in his Gospel. This word conveys "an active, continuous, and vital trust in Jesus"[6]—and more. Commentator Bruce Milne explains that the apostle's frequent use of "believe in" reflects John's concern for the dynamic nature of faith: "it involves much more than trust in Jesus or confidence in him, it is an acceptance of Jesus and of what he claims to be and a dedication of one's life to him." . . . "The sense must be that the believer throws himself upon his Lord in loving, self-abandoning faith and trust."[7]

We could even outline John's Gospel with this theme of belief, as Merrill Tenney shows:

1. The Prologue: The Proposal for Belief
   1:1-18
2. The Presentation for Belief
   1:19-4:54
3. The Reactions of Belief and Unbelief
   5:1-6:71
4. The Crystallization of Belief and Unbelief
   7:1-11:53
5. The Crisis of Belief and Unbelief
   11:54-12:50
6. The Assurance for Belief
   13:1-17:26
7. The Rejection by Unbelief
   18:1-19:42
8. The Vindication of Belief
   20:1-31
9. Epilogue: The Dedication of Belief
   21:1-25[8]

6. Edwin A. Blum, "John," in *The Bible Knowledge Commentary*, New Testament edition, ed. John F. Walvoord and Roy B. Zuck (Colorado Springs, Colo.: Chariot Victor Publishing, 1983), p. 270.

7. Bruce Milne, *The Message of John: Here Is Your King!*, The Bible Speaks Today Series (Downers Grove, Ill.: InterVarsity Press, 1993), p. 44. Milne quotes R. Brown, *The Gospel according to John* (New York, N.Y.: Doubleday, 1966), vol. 1, p. 513; and W. Turner, *Expository Times*, LXIV, 1952-53, p. 51.

8. Merrill C. Tenney, "The Gospel of John," in *The Expositor's Bible Commentary*, gen. ed. Frank E. Gaebelein (Grand Rapids, Mich.: Zondervan Publishing House, 1981), vol. 9, p. 13.

B. What is John's method? How does John go about presenting the evidence about Jesus so as to elicit our belief? Look again at 20:30–31 and you will see the clue.

> Many other *signs* therefore Jesus also performed in the presence of the disciples, which are not written in this book; but *these* have been written that you may believe that Jesus is the Christ, the Son of God; and that believing you may have life in His name. (emphasis added)

The word *sign, sēmeion* in Greek, refers to an act or miracle that is pregnant with meaning. It is not simply a display of supernatural power but a dynamic way of pointing out some aspect of the person of Christ. John records seven such signs, each a concrete demonstration that Jesus is God. These seven miracles all occur in Christ's *public ministry,* which lasts three years (chaps. 1–12). However, as public unbelief intensifies, the miracles cease, and for the few days before His Crucifixion, Jesus withdraws to a *private ministry* with the disciples (chaps. 13–21). John strategically places several keys to the structure of his Gospel where the attentive reader won't miss them. For example, one key, which we have already examined, is found in 20:30–31. A second key to understanding the structure of this book is found in 16:28:

> "I came forth from the Father, and have come into the world; I am leaving the world again, and going to the Father."

The Prologue (1:1–18), which we'll study in our next chapter, corresponds with Jesus' statement, "I came forth from the Father." Having "come into the world" covers 1:19–12:50. Jesus prepared His disciples for His "leaving the world again" in chapters 13–17. And from His arrest to His Resurrection and His final appearance to His disciples before His Ascension (chaps. 18–21), Jesus turned to go home "to the Father." (Another key to the theme and movement of John's Gospel is found in 1:11–12.)

A Concluding Application

From Shakespeare to Solzhenitsyn, the words of great writers reach across centuries and continents to grace us with the warm touch of kindness, the delicate touch of beauty, and the sure touch of truth. The Gospel of John is one of those books. It is not an exhaustive account of Christ's life. John's intent is not to write an epic on the life of Christ but to hold Jesus up so we can see

His glorious light and come out of the darkness. And when all is said and done, could there be a piece of literature with a more noble or eternal purpose? As C. S. Lewis stated:

> But the Christian knows from the outset that the salvation of a single soul is more important than the production or preservation of all the epics and tragedies in the world.[9]

What kind of things do you read? Sizzling best-sellers . . . the *Wall Street Journal* . . . *People* magazine? They may keep you enthralled, informed, and entertained, but none of them offer you what John has to offer. As we start our series on the Gospel of John, will you commit yourself to making it a priority on your reading list? It will change your life if you do—and that's a promise even Shakespeare couldn't make!

 Living Insights ━━━━━━━━━━━━━━━━

As you prepare to delve into the richness of John's Gospel and all it reveals about our Lord and Savior, Jesus Christ, take some time to get the big picture of this book. Study the outline provided at the beginning of this guide, but more than that, set aside a block of uninterrupted time to read straight through this Gospel. Ask the Lord to help you gain an understanding of the themes of this book and the mission of His Son. Notice, for example,

- how many times John contrasts light with dark,

- the deeds of light versus the deeds of darkness,

- fullness versus emptiness—what we hunger and thirst for and how Jesus provides,

- and the great overarching theme of life triumphing over death.

Jot down your observations, any insights the Lord gives you, and questions that may arise. This will give you a solid foundation for keeping John's whole purpose in mind as we examine smaller sections of his book throughout this guide and the next two. Happy reading!

9. C. S. Lewis, "Christianity and Literature," *Christian Reflections* (Grand Rapids, Mich.: William B. Eerdmans Publishing Co., 1968), p. 10.

Themes: _____

_____

_____

_____

_____

_____

_____

Contrasts: _____

_____

_____

_____

_____

_____

Observations and insights: _____

_____

_____

_____

_____

_____

Questions: _____

_____

_____

_____

_____

_____

Chapter 2
Prelude to Deity
John 1:1–18

In his classic *A Tale of Two Cities*, Charles Dickens summarizes the era of the French Revolution.

It was the best of times, it was the worst of times, it was the age of wisdom, it was the age of foolishness, it was the epoch of belief, it was the epoch of incredulity, it was the season of Light, it was the season of Darkness, it was the spring of hope, it was the winter of despair, we had everything before us, we had nothing before us, we were all going direct to Heaven, we were all going direct the other way.[1]

With this prologue Dickens preludes his drama. Before the curtain rises, he introduces us to some of the novel's major themes—prosperity and poverty, light and darkness, hope and despair.

John also introduces his Gospel with a prologue. R. C. H. Lenski, in his commentary on the Gospel of John, sees this eighteen-verse introduction as some of the most scintillating writing in the entire New Testament.

John's is the paragon among the Gospels, "the one, tender, real crown-Gospel of them all" (Luther), and the prolog is the central jewel set in pure gold.[2]

Like Dickens' introduction, John's prologue gives us a glimmer of the book's major themes: the deity of Christ; Christ as light and life; the world shrouded in darkness; the witness of John the Baptist; Israel's rejection of their Savior; Gentile acceptance; and examples of the glory, grace, and truth of Christ.

In this prologue, John establishes five arguments as to why Jesus was, in fact, divine: He was eternal (vv. 1–2); He was the Creator (vv. 3–5, 9); He gave spiritual life (vv. 10–13); He manifested glory (vv. 14–17); and He explained God (v. 18). Turning, then, to chapter 1, let's examine in depth John's prelude to deity.

I. The Son of God in Eternity
Alluding to the Creation account in Genesis 1:1, John establishes the deity of Christ by giving us a glimpse of Him before the foundation of the earth.

1. Charles Dickens, *A Tale of Two Cities* (Garden City, N.Y.: Nelson Doubleday, n.d.), p. 9.

2. R. C. H. Lenski, *The Interpretation of St. John's Gospel* (Columbus, Ohio: Wartburg Press, 1942), p. 26.

In the beginning was the Word, and the Word was
with God, and the Word was God. (John 1:1)

As we step into John's Gospel, we immediately slide through a
time tunnel that transports us to eternity past. In eternity—before
creation, before time itself—there existed the everlasting, triune
God. As Moses wrote,

Lord, Thou hast been our dwelling place in all
generations.
Before the mountains were born,
Or Thou didst give birth to the earth and the world,
Even from everlasting to everlasting, Thou art God.
(Ps. 90:1–2)

John introduces Jesus as "the Word," or in the Greek, *Logos*. Words
communicate, and that's precisely what Jesus did. Like a capstone
to the pyramid of prophets that preceded Him, Jesus was the final
spokesman for God (Heb. 1:1–2). From A to Z (Rev. 1:8), Jesus was
the divine alphabet spelling out God in such a way that even the
most elementary of us could grasp His essence. This Word, John
reveals to us, was *with* God, face-to-face, in eternity past. Yet in
some mysterious way, this Word was not only with God but *was*
God. Jesus was not simply the revealer of God but God Himself
revealed. Ivor Powell further illuminates this truth for us:

John taught that the Father and the Son were *one*; they
were co-equal and co-existent. The apostle believed that
when he listened to Jesus, he heard the voice and message of the Father. He was sure that when he gazed into
the face of Jesus, he saw the face of God.[3]

In Jesus we see the face . . . hear the voice . . . of God Himself!
And as God's first recorded words in Scripture were, "Let there be
light" (Gen. 1:3), so John next reveals that the Creator is none
other than Jesus Christ.

II. The Son of God at Creation

John 1:2–3 expands on the Son's role in creation.

He was in the beginning with God. All things came into
being by Him, and apart from Him nothing came into being that has come into being.

Two salient facts regarding Christ's deity are expressed here: (1)
Christ Himself was not created, and (2) all things were created by
Him. The Father was the architect, but Jesus was the primary agent
of creation (see also v. 10). First Corinthians 8:6 supports this
divine division of labor.

---

3. Ivor Powell, *Bible Names of Christ* (Grand Rapids, Mich.: Kregel Publications, 1988), p. 85.

Yet for us there is but one God, the Father, from whom
are all things, and we exist for Him; and one Lord, Jesus
Christ, by whom are all things, and we exist through Him.

Picking up on this idea, Colossians 1:16–17 reveals that Jesus is
not only the Creator of the universe but its Sustainer as well.

For by Him all things were created, both in the heavens
and on earth, visible and invisible, whether thrones or
dominions or rulers or authorities—all things have
been created by Him and for Him. And He is before all
things, and in Him all things hold together.

In John 1:4–5, John tells us something of the nature of this divine
Word.

In Him was life, and the life was the light of men. And the
light shines in the darkness, and the darkness did not
comprehend it.

Behind Christ's creative involvement was one crucial and dynamic
element: life! Turning from Christ's creative work to His saving
work, John shows us that just as Christ is the source of all physical
life, so is He also the source of all spiritual life.

The Meaning of Life

In Shakespeare's play *Macbeth*, the title character sums
up the emptiness of his evil life in this elegy for his wife.

Life's but a walking shadow, a poor player
That struts and frets his hour upon the stage
And then is heard no more. It is a tale
Told by an idiot, full of sound and fury,
Signifying nothing.[4]

Sounds like Solomon's life-under-the-sun philosophy,
doesn't it? Where "all is vanity" and "all things are weari-
some" (Eccles. 1:2, 8, 14).

In John's drama, however, life is not summed up in a
philosophy but in a person: "In *Him* was life, and the life was
the light of men" (John 1:4, emphasis added).

If you're looking for the essence of life in a philosophy,
you'll go away empty-handed. But if you come to the person
of Christ, you will find that *He* is life (14:6), and you'll walk
away with your arms full of His abundance (10:10b).

---

4. William Shakespeare, *Macbeth*, act 5, scene 5, lines 24–28.

Parenthetically, we are told of John the Baptist's ministry in relation to this life-giving Light.

> There came a man, sent from God, whose name was John. He came for a witness, that he might bear witness of the light, that all might believe through him. (vv. 6–7)

To prevent confusion, John distinguishes Jesus from His cousin John the Baptist by making clear each man's role: John as the messenger, Jesus as the Messiah.

> He [John] was not the light, but came that he might bear witness of the light.
> There was the true light which, coming into the world, enlightens every man. (vv. 8–9)

Four things can be said of *light* in these verses: First, it originates with Christ (v. 4). Second, it is not overpowered by darkness (v. 5). Third, it is unique—the *true* light (v. 9a). Fourth, it is universally available—it enlightens *everyone* (v. 9b). Christ offers life to enlighten every heart that draws close to Him.

Lighting Up Your Life

Jesus is truly the Light of the World. If you accept Him as your Savior, He can light up your life no matter how dark it may be.

> For God, who said, "Light shall shine out of darkness," is the One who has shone in our hearts to give the light of the knowledge of the glory of God in the face of Christ. (2 Cor. 4:6)

Where there is chaos, He can bring order. Where there is emptiness, He can bring fullness. Where there is darkness, He can bring light. And the darkness—no matter how deep—cannot overpower it!

III. The Son of God on Earth

In spite of the fact that Jesus offers Himself to everyone without exception, His light is shunned by many.

> He was in the world, and the world was made through Him, and the world did not know Him. He came to His own, and those who were His own did not receive Him. But as many as received Him, to them He gave the right to become children of God, even to those who believe in His name, who were born not of blood, nor of the will of the flesh, nor of the will of man, but of God. (John 1:10–13)

Like prisoners too long accustomed to the darkness of their cell—who shrink back with squinting eyes at the light of day—so many refused to step into the light of Christ (see 3:19). The world, in its hardness, stood as a defiant piece of sculpture, shunning its sculptor and refusing to acknowledge Christ as its maker. Not only did the creation "not know Him" (v. 10), but even Jesus' own people, the Jews, "did not receive Him" (v. 11). Fortunately, however, some did: a Samaritan woman here (chap. 4), an adulterous woman there (chap. 8), a lone blind man (chap. 9), and so on. Candle by candle, Jesus touched these dimly burning wicks of downtrodden humanity; and wick by wick, they, in turn, became lights to a world shivering in darkness (see Matt. 5:14–16).

IV. The Son of God Incarnate

Verse 14 describes the Incarnation—God becoming man in the person of Christ.

> And the Word became flesh, and dwelt[5] among us, and we beheld His glory, glory as of the only begotten from the Father, full of grace and truth. (see also Phil. 2:5–8)

In the Incarnation, deity funneled itself into humanity—the finest of wines into an ordinary earthenware vessel. Jesus traveled throughout Judea, Samaria, and Galilee teaching and healing— manifesting His glory so that the fragrant bouquet of deity filled the air with its aromatic presence. And, for a fleeting but festive moment, the world's parched lips tasted of the kingdom of God. Of this glorious Savior John the Baptist testified:

> John bore witness of Him, and cried out, saying, "This was He of whom I said, 'He who comes after me has higher rank than I, for He existed before me.'" For of His fulness we have all received, and grace upon grace. For the Law was given through Moses; grace and truth were realized through Jesus Christ. (vv. 15–17)

As a fountain fills the cups of eager street children, so Jesus fills us from His bottomless reservoir of grace and truth until at last our cups overflow.

V. The Son of God Explained the Father

When the divine sculptor became human clay, the abstractions of deity were explained in very concrete, human terms.

> No man has seen God at any time; the only begotten

---

5. Literally, *tabernacled*. This is an allusion to the tabernacle of Israel in the wilderness. Lesslie Newbigin helps us see the profound meaning in this imagery: "The consonants of the Greek word are those of the Hebrew word (*shekinah*) which denotes the presence and glory of God. The 'tent of meeting' was where God dwelt with his people and where his glory was seen (Ex. 40:34–38). . . . Now [in Jesus] . . . they have seen the glory of God tabernacling among men. . . . The fourth evangelist sees [Jesus'] whole ministry as a 'tabernacling' in which the disciples again and again had glimpses of his glory." *The Light Has Come: An Exposition of the Fourth Gospel* (Grand Rapids, Mich.: William B. Eerdmans Publishing Co., 1982), p. 8.

God, who is in the bosom of the Father, He has explained
Him. (v. 18)

Jesus explained God.[6] He was "the image of the invisible God"
(Col. 1:15), "the exact representation of His nature" (Heb. 1:3). On
this climactic note, John ends his prologue. He has carefully presented his evidence and shown that this Jesus of Nazareth, this
carpenter's son, could be none other than the Son of God—
because He's eternal (vv. 1–2), because He's the Creator (v. 3),
because He's the source of life (vv. 4–13), because He's God's
manifested glory (vv. 14–17), and because He's the unique explanation of God (v. 18). Jesus Christ is fully human *and* fully divine.

 Living Insights

Why is the deity of Jesus Christ so crucial to Christianity?[7]
Couldn't an ordinary, good man have died for our sins? Why must
we maintain that Jesus is eternal and not created? Why must we
insist that He is God?

Simply put, we'd have no Savior if Jesus had been less than deity.
No one but God could have lived out God's law perfectly, making
Him the spotless Lamb who took *our* place on the Cross and atoned
for *our* sins. Only God could grant forgiveness of sins and give us
new life.

So, you see, it was not enough for Jesus to be a good teacher or
moral example—He had to be God.

Is it any wonder that Christ's deity is one of the first doctrines
to be attacked by cults? For if they take away His deity, they take
away His atonement for our sins. Salvation then becomes a matter
of achieving God's favor through works. And that's exactly what
cults are—systems of righteousness by works.

In addition to what you've learned in John's inspired prologue,
look up some other key passages on Christ's deity. You'll not only
draw closer to your Savior, but you just might be better prepared to

---

6. The Greek word for "explained," *exegeomai*, "comes from the verb from which 'exegesis' is
derived, which means to 'explain' or 'interpret.' . . . The life and words of Jesus are more than
an announcement; they are an explanation of God's attitude toward men and of his purposes
for them." Merrill C. Tenney, "The Gospel of John," in *The Expositor's Bible Commentary*, gen.
ed. Frank E. Gaebelein (Grand Rapids, Mich.: Zondervan Publishing House, 1981), vol. 9, p. 34.

7. This Living Insight has been adapted from the study guide *God's Masterwork, Volume 4:
Matthew–1 Thessalonians*, coauthored by Gary Matlack and Bryce Klabunde, from the Bible-
teaching ministry of Charles R. Swindoll (Anaheim, Calif.: Insight for Living, 1997), pp. 49–50.

share the gospel with the next Mormon or Jehovah's Witness who knocks at your door. The following references will get you started.

Matthew 1:23 _____

_____

_____

Matthew 12:8 _____

_____

_____

Matthew 26:63–64 _____

_____

_____

Mark 2:1–12 _____

_____

_____

John 1:32–34 _____

_____

_____

John 6:68–69 _____

_____

_____

John 8:57–58 _____

_____

_____

John 10:30 _____

_____

_____

John 11:27 _____

John 20:28 _____

_____

_____

Philippians 2:5–11 _____

_____

_____

Colossians 1:15–20 _____

_____

_____

Titus 2:13 _____

_____

_____

Hebrews 1:1–4 _____

_____

_____

Chapter 3
A Man Sent from God
John 1:6–8, 15, 19–34

More than five hundred years ago, in the little hamlet of Ferrara, Italy, a baby boy was born into a noble family. His parents named him Girolamo Savonarola. Little did they realize that their baby would grow up to be a man sent from God.

From his earliest years, this keen, intelligent boy possessed an invincible love for God. By his own testimony, he was prepared to abandon life itself for the glory of Christ.

His saintly life was a mixture of loneliness and ruggedness. He deprived himself of every indulgence, content with only the hardest couch, the roughest clothing, the plainest food.

Savonarola lived in a time characterized by widespread corruption and wickedness in the church. The offices of bishop and cardinal were put up for auction and sold to the highest bidder. Immorality in its grossest forms was prevalent in monasteries and convents; even in local congregations it was displayed without shame. The church had become a den of vice and iniquity.

This so burdened the young priest that he spoke with fiery eloquence against these practices. For eight years he preached at the cathedral in Florence, pleading for purity of life and simplicity of worship.

Refusing to mix and mingle with officials of the church, he was resented and publicly assaulted by the clergy. Martyrdom appeared inevitable. Interrupting his devotions, church leaders broke into his monastery, dragged him into the streets, and locked him away in a loathsome dungeon. There he was tortured for weeks.

Finally, the day of his trial came. The church leaders were so determined to destroy him that one of the pope's commissioners wrote: "Put Savonarola to death, even if he were another John the Baptist."[1]

In a fit of unjust rage, they hanged him, set fire to his remains, and threw his ashes into the river Arno.

In Savonarola we find a perfect parallel to John the Baptist. Savonarola was a man sent from God to Italy; John the Baptist was a man

---

1. Philip Schaff, *History of the Christian Church* (Grand Rapids, Mich.: William B. Eerdmans Publishing Co., 1910), vol. 6, p. 710. For further study on Savonarola's life, consult pages 684–716 of the same volume.

sent from God to Israel. Both lived modestly and preached mightily. And both were forerunners, paving a highway for their Lord in a moral wilderness: Savonarola for the Reformation; John the Baptist for the kingdom of God.

I. Background of the Man Sent

John's parents were Zacharias and Elizabeth, both elderly people whom God graciously surprised with a baby, lifting the shame of barrenness and bestowing blessing instead (Luke 1:5–25). Luke informs us that, from his boyhood until the day of his public ministry, John lived in the deserts (v. 80). During this time, he was clothed in camel's hair, wore a leather belt, and ate a steady diet of locusts and wild honey (Mark 1:6). He gave a fire-and-brimstone call to repentance in order to prepare the way for Jesus (Matt. 3).

II. Characteristics of the Man Sent

Although his name was the most common of names, the man himself was the most uncommon of men.

A. He was human, but not ordinary. John 1:6 introduces this extraordinary man.

> There came a man, sent from God, whose name was John.

John was no angel, no spark of divinity—just a man. There was nothing significant about his name, unlike the names Immanuel and Jesus that were fraught with meaning. He was just John in a plain brown wrapper . . . but he was not ordinary. He was "sent from God," commissioned by the Almighty. He stood virtually alone and fit into no preformed mold. He was neither Pharisee nor Sadducee nor priest nor Levite nor scribe. He didn't sound like a priest . . . and he didn't smell like a saint.

B. He was a lamp, but not the light. Verse 7 tell us precisely why John came.

> He came for a witness, that he might bear witness of the light, that all might believe through him.

John came as a witness[2] with one goal in mind: to turn people around so they could see the light. His was not an office

---

2. The Greek noun for *witness* is *marturia*; the verb form is *martureo*. It "connotes the declaration or confirmation of facts or events." Of the 37 instances of the noun in the New Testament, 30 are found in John's writings; of the 76 instances of the verb, 47 are found in John's writings. Gerhard Kittel and Gerhard Friedrich, eds., *Theological Dictionary of the New Testament*, translated and abridged into one volume by Geoffrey W. Bromiley (1985; reprint, Grand Rapids, Mich.: William B. Eerdmans Publishing Co., 1992), pp. 566, 567. From the Greek root, *martus*, we get our word *martyr*, which means "a person who voluntarily suffers death as the penalty of witnessing to and refusing to renounce a religion" (*Merriam-Webster's Collegiate Dictionary*, 10th ed.). Such turned out to be the case for John the Baptist (Matt. 14:1–12).

embellished with the trappings of pomp and ceremony. He was no religious dignitary or published theologian. He was simply a beggar telling other beggars where to find bread, as verse 8 indicates.

> He was not the light, but came that he might bear witness of the light.

John was a lamp, but not the light; a wick, but not the flame. The "true light" that enlightens every man was Jesus (v. 9). John, then, saw himself in the shadow of the Savior.

> John bore witness of Him, and cried out, saying, "This was He of whom I said, 'He who comes after me has a higher rank than I, for He existed before me.'" (v. 15)

Some Personal Application

Most of us have had a variety of lamps in our homes over the years: desk lamps, swag lamps, chandeliers. Some have probably been fancy, fashioned in brass or silver. Some have been made of stained glass; others, crystal. Some, too, may have been very common, like a simple porcelain closet fixture.

Whatever, the important thing is the light, not the lamp. It's the glow in the bulb that lights up a room, not the shine on the brass or crystal.

Are you exhibiting Christ in your life as the true Light of the World, or is the ornamentation of your lamp the main thing people see? Is His light radiating through your life, or is it being obstructed by a cumbersome lampshade of sin?

C. **He was a voice, but not the Word.** Like the relationship between a singer's voice and the song's lyrics, John was simply "a voice of one crying in the wilderness" (v. 23), while Jesus was the Word of God (vv. 1–2).

> And this is the witness of John, when the Jews sent to him priests and Levites from Jerusalem to ask him, "Who are you?" And he confessed, and did not deny, and he confessed, "I am not the Christ." And they asked him, "What then? Are you Elijah?" And he said, "I am not." "Are you the Prophet?"[3]

---

3. Malachi predicted that Elijah would come to herald the appearance of the Messiah (Mal. 4:5). The synoptic writers persistently identified John with Elijah (Matt. 11:14; 17:12; Mark 9:11–13), which poses a problem in light of John's denial in John 1:21. However, the problem is resolved when it is understood that John is denying a *literal* identification with Elijah, while the synoptic

And he answered, "No." They said then to him, "Who are you, so that we may give an answer to those who sent us? What do you say about yourself?" He said, "I am a voice of one crying in the wilderness, 'Make straight the way of the Lord,' as Isaiah the prophet said." (vv. 19–23)

Why did one have to make straight the way of the Lord? What did John mean by these words? The quote is from Isaiah 40:3, and the imagery is explained by Merrill Tenney in his commentary on John's Gospel.

> The imagery was taken from the days when there were no paved roads, only tracks across the fields. If a king were to travel, the road must be built and smoothed out that the royal chariot might not find the traveling unduly rough, nor be swamped in the mire.[4]

Just as a special road had to be leveled when a king desired to cross a desert, so a path was to be paved by John for the Messiah.

Highway through the Heart

To describe Israel's spiritual condition at the coming of the Messiah, John the Baptist chooses the metaphor of a wilderness—a place that is desolate, dry, and barren. What metaphor would he be inclined to choose if he had to describe your heart? Would it be a wilderness . . . a fallow field . . . a meadow . . . or an Eden?

The highway to heaven is paved over prepared hearts. Hearts that are repentant. Hearts that are soft. Hearts that are fertile. Isaiah makes it clear that the rough terrain in our hearts needs to be smoothed before the Lord can come near.

A voice is calling,
"Clear the way for the Lord in the wilderness;

---

writers are *spiritually* identifying John with the prophet. Compare the angel of the Lord's words about John in Luke 1:17: "And it is he who will go as a forerunner before Him *in the spirit and power* of Elijah . . ." (emphasis added). Also, as D. A. Carson notes, John may simply not have detected "as much significance in his own ministry as Jesus did." *The Gospel according to John* (Grand Rapids, Mich.: William B. Eerdmans Publishing Co., 1991), p. 143. Regarding the reference to "the Prophet," see Deuteronomy 18:5.

4. Merrill C. Tenney, *John: The Gospel of Belief* (Grand Rapids, Mich.: William B. Eerdmans Publishing Co., 1948), p. 79.

> Make smooth in the desert a highway for our
>   God.
> Let every valley be lifted up,
> And every mountain and hill be made low;
> And let the rough ground become a plain,
> And the rugged terrain a broad valley."
> (Isa. 40:3–4)
> When you read your Bible and pray, have you first
> cleared the way for the Lord in the wilderness of your
> heart? When you worship, have you first made smooth
> in the desert a highway for your God? If God seems
> distant in your life, maybe you need to do a little road-
> work of repentance in order to prepare the way for Him.

D. **He was useful, but not indispensable.** Still confused, those
sent by the Pharisees probed further.

> And they asked him, and said to him, "Why then are
> you baptizing, if you are not the Christ, nor Elijah,
> nor the Prophet?" John answered them saying, "I
> baptize in water, but among you stands One whom
> you do not know. It is He who comes after me, the
> thong of whose sandal I am not worthy to untie."
> These things took place in Bethany beyond the Jor-
> dan, where John was baptizing. (John 1:25–28)

John's humility can readily be seen in verse 27, the background
to the verse bringing it into even sharper focus. There is a
rabbinic saying that John probably had in mind when he spoke
of Jesus' sandal. "Every service which a slave performs for
his master shall a disciple do for his teacher except the loosing
of his sandal-thong."[5] John was willing to stoop to the lowest
level of servility in deference to the Messiah.

E. **He was a witness, but not an object of worship.** A witness
does not tell his own story but testifies only to what he has
seen and heard. In verses 29–33, John directed others' attention to Jesus.

> The next day he saw Jesus coming to him, and
> said, "Behold, the Lamb of God who takes away the
> sin of the world! This is He on behalf of whom I
> said, 'After me comes a Man who has a higher rank

---

5. Quoted by Leon Morris, in *The Gospel according to John,* rev. ed., The New International
Commentary on the New Testament Series (Grand Rapids, Mich.: William B. Eerdmans Publishing Co., 1995), p. 124.

than I, for He existed before me.' And I did not recognize Him, but in order that He might be manifested to Israel, I came baptizing in water." And John bore witness saying, "I have beheld the Spirit descending as a dove out of heaven, and He remained upon Him. And I did not recognize Him, but He who sent me to baptize in water said to me, 'He upon whom you see the Spirit descending and remaining upon Him, this is the one who baptizes in the Holy Spirit.'"

The voice made ready the way of the Word. The confronter of sins heralded the One who takes all sin away. The "man sent from God" bowed to the One who came as God in the flesh. The forerunner needed God to reveal the One he was running before. The water-baptizer pointed to the Spirit-baptizer. And, finally, this priest's son testified that Jesus was indeed the very Son of God:

"And I have seen, and have borne witness that this is the Son of God." (v. 34)

III. Marks of God-Sent People Today

Leadership has its own particular perils: pride, egotism, envy, jealousy, the compromises of popularity, assumed infallibility, illusions of indispensability, and so on. But John gave a timeless principle for us in chapter 3, verse 30.

"He must increase, but I must decrease."

The true qualities of people sent by God are that they exalt the One who sent them, and they diminish the one who is sent.

Second Wind for Savonarola

Savonarola had an incredible experience when he went from Genoa to Florence. Believing that God had sent him to minister to the corrupt San Marco monastery, Savonarola journeyed there, only to collapse with fatigue at the base of the mountain range that led to the monastery.

Despairing of life, Savonarola was visited by a stranger. Whether the stranger was real or a vision or an angel, we don't know. But the story has the visitor feeding the discouraged traveler, giving him rest, and encouraging him.

The stranger helped Savonarola reach the gate of the monastery. Once there, the stranger is reported to have said, "And now, Savonarola, remember to do that for which God has sent thee"; then to have left.

Being a voice in a moral wilderness can be a lonely and discouraging experience. It's easy for fatigue and despair to

set in. But many of you have felt the call to be that voice—
in your family, at your school, where you work.

If that's the case, and you're feeling faint and discouraged,
feeling you can't go on, I hope this study has given you some
much-needed nourishment and rest. Now, let me be that
stranger and encourage you to get up and "remember to do
that for which God has sent thee."

Living Insights

What is John the Baptist's message for us today? Like Abel,
"though he is dead, he still speaks" (Heb. 11:4). Let's listen to the
testimony of his life throughout all the Gospels and hear what he
is saying.

His first words in Matthew's account are, "Repent, for the
kingdom of heaven is at hand" (3:2). From verses 3 and 8, what does
it mean to repent?

_____

_____

_____

_____

Why is repenting of our sins so crucial to welcoming the kingdom
of heaven? What would John have us avoid (see vv. 7, 9–12)?

_____

_____

_____

Sin opposes, or puts up roadblocks, to God's coming into our lives.
We turn away from God instead of toward Him when we sin. Are there
any paths you need to make straight in order to restore fellowship
with the Lord? Take some time to address them right now.

_____

_____

_____

_____

In Mark's Gospel, John the Baptist is the very first person we meet. After Isaiah's prophecy introduces him (Isa. 40:3), Mark gives a quick summary of his ministry and appearance. Then Mark lets the Baptizer speak (v. 7). He makes a different impression in this Gospel than in Matthew's. What character quality do his words reveal?

Does this quality characterize your relationship with Christ? Sometimes in our American Christian culture we can become overly familiar with Jesus, treating Him as a mere "buddy." What does John's witness tell you about awe, reverence, and humility? How can you cultivate these qualities? How can you make an impact to help Christianity grow past the "buddy syndrome"?

In Luke's Gospel, we meet John through the words of an angel of the Lord. What does the angel say John will do (Luke 1:16–17)?

Where Matthew stressed the urgent need of repentance in the context of coming judgment, Luke celebrates the restorative outcome of turning our hearts back to God. Joy, gladness, and rejoicing surround John's ministry in Luke, rather than the severe austerity Matthew communicates. How do you reconcile these two approaches? How do Zacharias' words in Luke 1:76–79 relate with Matthew's perspective (compare Luke 3:2b–17)?

Luke's words feel better, but both Matthew's and Luke's accounts of John's words are "gospel" (Luke 3:18)—good news. How are the more stern words also good news?

_____

_____

_____

Even a forerunner's certainty can waver (Luke 7:19–23). Where does John's witness tell us to bring our doubts?

_____

_____

In the Gospel of John, what is the dominant descriptive word for the Baptizer (see vv. 7–8, 15, 19, 32, 34; 3:26; 5:33)?

_____

John was not the Light, but he pointed to the Light; he affirmed the truth about Jesus being the Light. Do you consciously determine—have as an overarching principle of your life—to reflect the reality of who Jesus is in what you say and do? In what areas do you need to be reminded of your role as Christ's witness? When you're driving, for example? When you have to deal with an unlovely, unthinking person? When you've been wronged?

_____

_____

_____

_____

Maybe we could sum up John's message in each of the Gospels like this: In Matthew, "Be holy." In Mark, "Be humble." In Luke, "Be reconciled." In John, "Be a reflector of Christ." Let this man sent from God help you make any rough roads in your life smooth, won't you? If you do, the eyes of your heart will be prepared to see God's tender mercies and life according to His way of peace (Luke 1:78–79).

Chapter 4

Five Who Followed in Faith

John 1:35–51

Religious art has, for centuries, cast the disciples of Christ into porcelain molds—museum-quality reproductions, polished and protected. Glossed over with the smooth glaze of reverence, the flaws of the Twelve have largely been forgotten by time. But the people whom Jesus called were hardly porcelain-perfect saints.

The men and women to whom Jesus offered this gift were ordinary human beings, faulted and flawed, just like the rest of us. He gave his disciples no job descriptions; he did not disqualify Mary Magdalene because she had been afflicted with seven demons; he did not spend a lot of time looking for the most qualified people, the most adult. Instead, he chose people who were still childlike enough to leave the known comforts of the daily world, the security of their jobs, their reasonable way of life, to follow him.[1]

In this chapter, we will take a closer look at five of those men—five who followed in faith.

I. General Orientation

Let's survey the ground we will cover in the last half of John 1 before we look at each man who followed Christ.

A. Time. Verses 29–51 describe a three-day period. Note the words "next day" repeated in verses 29, 35, and 43.

B. Structure. The passage is simple and straightforward in style, with a definite structure emerging from John's observation of each of the men named. In each case, there is an evangelistic approach that creates interest and then a conversation with Christ that leads to a life-changing decision.

C. People. Only four are actually named: Andrew, Peter, Philip, and Nathanael. The fifth, cloaked in the authorial garb of anonymity, is most likely John. All are ordinary, T-shirt-and-blue-jeans types—working men, primed for a challenge.

II. Specific Exposition

As we look at the calling of each disciple, we can see both similarities and differences in the way they came to follow Christ.

---

1. Madeleine L'Engle, *Walking on Water: Reflections on Faith and Art* (Wheaton, Ill.: Harold Shaw Publishers, 1980), p. 89.

A. Andrew and John. The first men to follow Jesus were Andrew and John. The scene is staged to spotlight a transference of allegiance from John the Baptist to Jesus—which fulfilled the Baptist's mission of pointing to the One whose ministry would supersede his own (vv. 26–27).[2]

> Again the next day John was standing with two of his disciples, and he looked upon Jesus as He walked, and said, "Behold, the Lamb of God!" And the two disciples heard him speak, and they followed Jesus. (vv. 35–37)

Notice the structure of the account: first the *approach* (v. 35), then the *message* (v. 36), and finally the *response* (v. 37). John's ministry of baptizing and preaching to the crowds at the Jordan is an example of *mass evangelism,* of which these two disciples were a part. The message was that Jesus was "the Lamb of God."[3] The result—they followed Christ.

A Time to Reflect

In John Baillie's devotional classic, *A Diary of Private Prayer*, the author asks God to keep him "loyal to every hallowed memory of the past."[4]

Do you remember the time when you, like Andrew and John, first realized that Jesus was the sacrificial lamb who died in your place? Remember when you came to Him by faith and He embraced you with forgiveness? Angels rejoiced in heaven and you were given new life . . . a second chance . . . a fresh start for all eternity.

It may have been years ago, but you can probably still remember every detail of that day. Take a few minutes to reflect on that time and hallow that moment in your memory.

A more personal picture of these two fledgling disciples is folded away in verses 38–39.

> And Jesus turned, and beheld them following, and said to them, "What do you seek?" And they said

---

2. See Bruce Milne, *The Message of John: Here Is Your King!,* The Bible Speaks Today Series (Downers Grove, Ill.: InterVarsity Press, 1993), p. 56.

3. The Passover lamb was a foreshadowing of Christ (compare Exod. 12 with 1 Cor. 5:7; also compare Isa. 53:7 with 1 Pet. 1:19). For a fuller discussion, consult Leon Morris, *The Word Was Made Flesh: John 1–5,* vol. 1 of *Reflections on the Gospel of John* (Grand Rapids, Mich.: Baker Book House, 1986), pp. 35–42.

4. John Baillie, *A Diary of Private Prayer* (New York, N.Y.: Charles Scribner's Sons, 1949), p. 9.

to Him, "Rabbi (which translated means Teacher), where are You staying?" He said to them, "Come, and you will see." They came therefore and saw where He was staying; and they stayed with Him that day, for it was about the tenth hour.

Isn't Jesus' question penetrating? "What are you looking for, Andrew and John? What do you want?" With this question Jesus not only asks them to be aware of their motives, probing them "to find out whether they were motivated by idle curiosity or by a real desire to know him."[5] But He also goes deeper, compelling them to "articulate what they really want in life."[6] It's not an easy question, and Andrew and John wanted to abide with Jesus for a while to figure out how they would answer. So Jesus graciously invited them to more intimate surroundings, where they could talk and get to know Him.

B. Simon Peter. Having spent the day with Jesus, Andrew leaves convinced that He is the Messiah. What is his response? To tell his brother and bring him to Jesus. Leon Morris notes an interesting facet of Andrew's character: "Each time we meet Andrew in this Gospel he is bringing someone to Jesus (6:8; 12:22), a consistency worth noting."[7] He may have lived in his brother's shadow (note the way John describes him in 1:40), but he became and remained a faithful, valuable follower of Christ's in his own right. Let's see how Jesus receives Andrew's brother.

> One of the two who heard John speak, and followed Him, was Andrew, Simon Peter's brother. He found first his own brother Simon, and said to him, "We have found the Messiah" (which translated means Christ). He brought him to Jesus. Jesus looked at him, and said, "You are Simon the son of John; you shall be called Cephas" (which translated means Peter). (vv. 40–42)

What word comes to mind when you think of Simon Peter? *Impulsive? Vocal? Rash?* Perhaps all of these. Yet when Jesus met Simon, the word that came to His mind connoted an image

5. Merrill C. Tenney, "The Gospel of John," in *The Expositor's Bible Commentary,* gen. ed. Frank E. Gaebelein (Grand Rapids, Mich.: Zondervan Publishing House, 1981), vol. 9, p. 40.

6. D. A. Carson, *The Gospel according to John* (Grand Rapids, Mich.: William B. Eerdmans Publishing Co., 1991), p. 155.

7. Leon Morris, *The Gospel according to John,* rev. ed., The New International Commentary on the New Testament Series (Grand Rapids, Mich.: William B. Eerdmans Publishing Co., 1995), p. 140.

both solid and stable—Cephas, the "rock." Jesus not only saw the man Peter would become but also knew that He would make him what He called him to be (see Phil. 1:6; 1 Thess. 5:24; Heb. 12:2; Jude 24).[8] Notice, too, the sequence of events. The approach was one of *personal evangelism,* brother to brother (vv. 40–41a). The message was, "We have found the Messiah"[9] (v. 41b). The response was Peter's face-to-face encounter with Jesus, giving him the encouragement he needed to follow Christ (v. 42).

Seeing beyond the Rough Edges

Catching a glimpse of Peter's life under the magnifying glass of Scripture, we see a lot of rough edges on that stone. At times he is hardheaded, and at times, even abrasive.

But Jesus was able to see beyond all that—beyond the rough edges to the precious stone beneath, beyond the stubbornness to the stability.

Jesus had a jeweler's eye for spotting a diamond in the rough. Do you? Can you see the potential in others? Can you see beneath all the rough edges to the precious stone hidden within your child? Can you spot that jewel-in-the-making when you look at your spouse or your friend?

Oftentimes, a simple recognition of the presence of the jewel is all the encouragement people need to start chipping away at their own rough edges, bringing that precious stone to light.

C. Philip. Without John's record, Philip would have slipped between the cracks of biblical history, and his name would have been lost forever. But in John's Gospel we find a brief, yet revealing, character sketch of Philip. We see him as logical, somewhat pessimistic, and having a little difficulty stepping out in faith (see 6:1–7; 12:20–22; 14:7–9). Maybe that's why Jesus took the initiative in calling him.

> The next day He purposed to go forth into Galilee. And He found Philip. And Jesus said to him, "Follow Me." Now Philip was from Bethsaida, of the city of Andrew and Peter. (1:43–44)

---

8. Carson, *The Gospel according to John,* p. 156.

9. For the benefit of his non-Jewish readers, John translates the Hebrew term *Messiah* with the Greek *Christos* (from the root *chrio,* meaning "to anoint"). It means "the anointed one," linking Jesus to prophets (1 Kings 19:16), priests (Exod. 29:4–7), and kings (1 Sam. 16:1–13; 1 Kings 1:39). See Carson, *The Gospel according to John,* p. 156.

Christ's approach with Philip was *cold-contact evangelism.* Apparently, they had never met before, and Jesus confronted him directly on the street. The message was "Follow Me." Simple and straightforward. No high-pressure sales pitch. No recruiting posters. No campaign promises. Just Jesus, calmly bidding, "Follow Me." The response, seen in the next verses, was that Philip did follow Him.

D. Nathanael. Immediately and enthusiastically, Philip found Nathanael and told him the good news.

> Philip found Nathanael and said to him, "We have found Him of whom Moses in the Law and also the Prophets wrote, Jesus of Nazareth, the son of Joseph." And Nathanael said to him, "Can any good thing come out of Nazareth?" Philip said to him, "Come and see." (vv. 45–46)

Keenly critical, Nathanael responds with unguarded candor— "Nazareth? That's not in any prophecy. Come on, Philip, get real." Yet his skepticism was honest; his brusqueness, without hypocrisy. And these were the very jewels Jesus saw sparkling beneath his skepticism.

> Jesus saw Nathanael coming to Him, and said of him, "Behold, an Israelite indeed, in whom is no guile!" (v. 47)[10]

This perceptive greeting astonished Nathanael. He had never seen Jesus before and was quite sure that Jesus had never seen him.

> Nathanael said to Him, "How do You know me?" Jesus answered and said to him, "Before Philip called you, when you were under the fig tree, I saw you." (v. 48)

Philip's approach to Nathanael resembles Andrew's approach to Peter. However, it is possible that the Word of God played an integral part in Nathanael's coming to Christ—perhaps we could call it *Word evangelism.* The Jewish Talmud encouraged sincere, searching Jews to seek out places of solitude where they could pray, meditate, and study the Scriptures. Rabbinic writings give evidence that scholars and students often studied under shade trees. Perhaps Nathanael was digging into the

---

10. The Hebrew word for *guile* originally referred to the bait used in catching fish. In time the word came to denote any cunning device or deceptive ploy. The Greek translation of the Old Testament uses *guile* in its description of Jacob when he deceived Isaac (Gen. 27:35). Some even translate Jesus' words as, "An Israelite in whom there is no Jacob." See Morris, *The Gospel according to John,* p. 145.

Old Testament prophecies of the Messiah at the very time Jesus had seen him. That conjecture would certainly account for Philip's reference to the Law and the Prophets and for Nathanael's enthusiastic response when he met Christ.

> Nathanael answered Him, "Rabbi, You are the Son of God; You are the King of Israel." (v. 49)

Echoes from the Old Testament

The entire Old Testament stands on tiptoe, anticipating the coming of the Messiah, God's anointed King of Israel (Ps. 2; 110).

In 1 Chronicles 28:9, David wisely counsels his son Solomon concerning his relationship with God: "If you seek Him, He will let you find Him."

Certainly this held true for Nathanael.

Certainly it can hold true for you as well.

In response, Jesus promises His new disciple that he will see even greater things than Jesus' foreknowledge of him.

> Jesus answered and said to him, "Because I said to you that I saw you under the fig tree, do you believe? You shall see greater things than these." And He said to him, "Truly, truly, I say to you, you shall see the heavens opened, and the angels of God ascending and descending on the Son of Man." (vv. 50–51)

Alluding again to Jacob, Jesus tells the worshipful Nathanael that he will see angels "ascending and descending" as they did on a ladder from earth to heaven in the patriarch's dream (Gen. 28:12). Notice, though, that Jesus omits the ladder, indicating that He Himself is now the link between heaven and earth—He "is the new and supreme point at which God and humanity intersect."[11] In Him the heavens will remain open as He represents God to us and us to God. What a wonderful message to share!

---

11. Milne, *The Message of John,* p. 60.

☀ *Living Insights*

Did you notice something unique in Jesus' approach to these five men who followed Him? It concerns something He didn't do, actually, in contrast to something we often do. It's especially clear in His encounters with Peter and Nathanael. Any ideas?

That's right, He didn't camp on their sins. He didn't harangue them about being lost and going to hell.

Instead, He told them about the good He saw in them.

That's different, isn't it? Bruce Milne observes,

> Peter, the second recruit identified, is addressed by Jesus in terms of the person he was to become. . . . It is striking how regularly Jesus approached people from the perspective of their potential. Our concern to declare the sin and fallenness of those we witness to (which has its place, cf. "though you are evil," Lk. 11:13) must not inhibit our recognition of the possibilities of grace ("know how to give good gifts," Lk. 11:13). The vision of future potential can be a deeply effective means to the realizing of that potential.[12]

How attuned are you to the "possibilities of grace" in others? What do you see first in people: their good qualities or their flaws? Why?

_____

_____

_____

_____

_____

How much of your "people vision" is shaped by God's love for all His people?

_____

_____

_____

12. Milne, *The Message of John,* p. 59.

Let's get a bit more specific. Think of someone close to you—perhaps your spouse or one of your parents, children, siblings, or friends—in whom you have trouble seeing much good sometimes. Now put on the glasses of God's love and grace. What do you see? List all the good qualities you can think of.

_____

_____

_____

_____

_____

Does this impact your attitude toward this person? How?

_____

_____

_____

_____

Make a point this week to share the good you see in this person either face-to-face or in a letter he or she could keep. And remember some other words of Jesus:

"However you want people to treat you, so treat them, for this is the Law and the Prophets." (Matt. 7:12)

Let's follow Jesus' lead and start looking for those possibilities of grace in ourselves and in others!

Chapter 5

Wine . . . Coins . . . and Signs

John 2

In 1980, wine buyers from all over the world gathered at the twelfth annual Heublein Rare Wine Auction in San Francisco. At the auction, a restaurant owner who had vowed to get "the finest bottle of wine in the world" spent $31,000 for a vintage 1822 bottle of Chateau Lafite Rothschild.

The well-heeled audience of more than three hundred wine connoisseurs gasped and applauded as the auctioneer slammed his gavel on the podium, ending the brisk, three-minute competition to capture this prized wine.[1] Valued not only for its rarity but also for its incomparable taste, Chateau Lafite continues to break auction records year after year.

But the world's finest wine was not made in the vineyards of France, nor was it served in the finest international restaurants. It was made and served at an unpretentious wedding in Cana of Galilee—two thousand years ago. And that wine is valued to this day, not for its rarity, but for what it reveals about its maker . . . Jesus Christ.

I. Outlining the Chapter

The purpose of John's Gospel, remember, is to demonstrate that Jesus of Nazareth is the Son of God. In John 2, the author forcefully accomplishes this. But before we get into the individual verses, let's understand how this chapter fits within the framework of what has occurred before.

A. Chronologically. Chapter 2 begins with the words "And on the third day." This raises the question: the third day of what? If you trace John's narrative in chapter 1, the chronology may become a little clearer. The first day of the account is found in 1:19; the second, 1:29; the third, 1:35; the fourth, 1:43. Therefore, the "third day" in 2:1 would be the third day after Philip's and Nathanael's conversions in 1:43–51.

B. Geographically. Mapped out in the first two chapters, Jesus' preaching itinerary takes Him to Bethany (1:28), Galilee (1:43), Cana of Galilee (2:1), Capernaum (2:12), and Jerusalem (2:13, 23).

C. Analytically. As we take a more analytical look at our passage, we find three incidents—involving wine, coins, and signs— each significant.

---

1. "Memphis Man Spends $31,000 on 'Finest Wine,'" *Fort Worth Star-Telegram,* May 29, 1980.

II. Understanding the Issues

The three incidents in John 2—wine at the wedding (vv. 1–11), coins in the temple (vv. 14–17), and signs for the Jews (vv. 18–22) —reveal different facets of Jesus' divine character.

A. Wine at the wedding. First-century weddings differed greatly from today's. A one-year betrothal period preceded the actual ceremony. Much more binding than modern-day engagements, only a bill of divorcement could break it. At the end of the wedding day, the groom and his friends came to get the bride at her parents' house. "A procession then set out from the bride's home to the couple's new home, and the dark roadway would be lit with oil lamps held by wedding guests."[2] Singing and music accompanied the newly married couple along the way, and when they arrived, the wedding banquet began. This prolonged feast, mixing ceremony with celebration, lasted as long as a week. Hospitality was extremely important—the hosts not only took great care to provide whatever the guests needed but "were legally required to provide a feast of a certain standard."[3]

1. The incident. The wedding feast, apparently large,[4] is recounted in verses 1–11.

> And on the third day there was a wedding in Cana of Galilee, and the mother of Jesus was there; and Jesus also was invited, and His disciples, to the wedding. And when the wine gave out, the mother of Jesus said to Him, "They have no wine." And Jesus said to her, "Woman, what do I have to do with you? My hour has not yet come." His mother said to the servants, "Whatever He says to you, do it." Now there were six stone water-cools set there for the Jewish custom of purification, containing twenty or thirty gallons each. Jesus said to them, "Fill the water-cools with water." And they filled them up to the brim. And He

2. Ralph Gower, *The New Manners and Customs of Bible Times* (Chicago, Ill.: Moody Press, 1987), p. 66.

3. Leon Morris, *The Gospel according to John*, rev. ed., The New International Commentary on the New Testament Series (Grand Rapids, Mich.: William B. Eerdmans Publishing Co., 1995), p. 158.

4. Verse 6 notes six stone water pots, containing 20 to 30 gallons each. Based on a 25-gallon average, the combined total would have been 150 gallons. At servings of 1 cup each, this would make 2,400 servings . . . and this was after the feast had been underway for some time.

said to them, "Draw some out now, and take it to the headwaiter." And they took it to him. And when the headwaiter tasted the water which had become wine, and did not know where it came from (but the servants who had drawn the water knew), the headwaiter called the bridegroom, and said to him, "Every man serves the good wine first, and when men have drunk freely, then that which is poorer; you have kept the good wine until now." This beginning of His signs Jesus did in Cana of Galilee, and manifested His glory, and His disciples believed in Him.

2. The issue. The real issue at the wedding was not the wine running out but who replenished it. Jesus had the servants fill six stone water-cools—which were used for ritual purification purposes under Jewish law—with water. Then He transformed that water into the best of wine— "You have kept the good wine until now," the headwaiter exclaimed (v. 10). Commentator Leon Morris highlights the meaning of this first of Jesus' signs[5]:

> This particular miracle signifies that there is a transforming power associated with Jesus. He changes the water of Judaism into the wine of Christianity, the water of Christlessness into the wine of the richness and the fullness of eternal life in Christ, the water of the law into the wine of the gospel.[6]

In an instant, Jesus' disciples saw proof of His divine power as Creator, as the One through whom "all thing came into being" (1:3a), and as the One who superseded Moses' law with God's own grace (vv. 16–17). In Jesus they saw God's glory (v. 14), and they believed in Him (2:11). Certainly, it is well within the scope of Jesus' power to transform the quality of our lives as well, making us fit vessels to display His glory (see Matt. 5:16; 2 Cor. 4:5–7).

---

5. Unlike the other Gospel writers, John uses the word *sign* rather than *miracle* or *wonder* to point beyond the supernatural miracle to what it signifies. Signs, then, are "special actions by Jesus which reveal his glory to those who believe and which confront others with the need to decide about Jesus." Bruce Milne, *The Message of John: Here Is Your King!*, The Bible Speaks Today Series (Downers Grove, Ill.: InterVarsity Press, 1993), p. 62.

6. Morris, *The Gospel according to John*, p. 155.

B. Coins in the temple. John 2:12–13 form a transition to the next incident in chapter 2.

> After this He went down to Capernaum, He and His mother, and His brothers, and His disciples; and there they stayed a few days.
>
> And the Passover of the Jews was at hand, and Jesus went up to Jerusalem.

Passover—the greatest of all Jewish feasts.[7] By Jewish law, every male within fifteen miles of Jerusalem was required to make the journey to the sacred city for the celebration. And since every Jew dreamed of celebrating at least one Passover in Jerusalem, many more pilgrims came from outside that radius, swelling the city with as many as $2\frac{1}{4}$ million visitors each year. Opportunistic Jewish officials put a sharp pencil to the situation and figured out how to make it a more rewarding stay—for themselves, that is, not for the travelers.

1. The incident. When Jesus went to the temple courtyard, the scene infuriated Him.

> And He found in the temple those who were selling oxen and sheep and doves, and the money changers seated. (v. 14)

Every Jew over nineteen was required to pay a temple tax, which could only be paid in Galilean or sanctuary shekels—hence, the need for money changers. The corruption, however, was not in the system but in the exorbitant rate these unscrupulous financiers charged. Adding to the corruption was the way sacrifices were approved. A fee was charged to inspect all animals brought to the temple for sacrifice. Most of the time, the inspectors found the animal blemished in some way, disqualifying it as a legitimate offering. This forced the out-of-town traveler to purchase an "approved" animal at the temple for often ten to twenty times the fair market value.[8] No wonder Christ was enraged.

> And He made a scourge of cords, and drove them all out of the temple, with the sheep and the oxen; and He poured out the coins of the money changers, and overturned their tables; and to those who were selling the doves He said, "Take these things away; stop making My

---

7. Passover is a time of remembrance for when God delivered Israel from Egypt (see Exod. 12).

8. See William Barclay, *The Gospel of John*, rev. ed., The Daily Study Bible Series (Philadelphia, Pa.: Westminster Press, 1975), pp. 108–14.

Father's house a house of merchandise." His
disciples remembered that it was written, "Zeal
for Thy house will consume me." (vv. 15–17)

2. **The issue.** This incident is clearly an account of removing
from the temple those who were desecrating it. The issue
is the sanctity of the temple, the dwelling place of deity.
Today God dwells in the temple of our physical bodies
(see 1 Cor. 6:19–20). The implications of this are enor-
mous. We are not to allow the place where God dwells to
become a house of merchandise—a loud, busy, deceptive
place. It must be a place of prayer . . . a place of
sanctity . . . a place of worship, where we can commune
with God in spirit and in truth (John 4:23).

Cleansing the Temple

What do you allow to enter your "temple"? Does
it enhance God's dwelling place—or does it defile
and desecrate it?

If the latter, expect a cleansing visit from Christ, because He has a zeal for God's honor and a love for us
that won't allow anything but the best (Heb. 12:5–11).

C. **Signs for the Jews.** The incident of Christ cleansing the temple
brought Psalm 69:9 to the sensitive minds of the disciples. But
the disgruntled merchandisers of faith—not so perceptive—
wanted a little more positive identification. They wanted some
authoritative sign (compare 1 Cor. 1:22).

1. **The incident.** Jesus not only overturned the money changers' business tables, He upended their mental tables as well.

The Jews therefore answered and said to Him,
"What sign do You show to us, seeing that You
do these things?" Jesus answered and said to
them, "Destroy this temple, and in three days
I will raise it up." The Jews therefore said, "It
took forty-six years to build this temple, and
will You raise it up in three days?" But He was
speaking of the temple of His body. When
therefore He was raised from the dead, His
disciples remembered that He said this; and
they believed the Scripture, and the word
which Jesus had spoken. (John 2:18–22)

2. **The issue.** Sidestepping Jesus' demand to cleanse the
temple and restore true worship, the Jews instead asked
for a sign; what they needed, however, was salvation. "It

is a demand for the visible at the expense of the ethical."[9] The issue was not what they wanted to see; it was what they needed to believe. This shallow type of faith, which substantiated itself on signs, prompted John to write the following postscript.

> Now when He was in Jerusalem at the Passover, during the feast, many believed in His name, beholding His signs which He was doing. But Jesus, on His part, was not entrusting Himself to them, for He knew all men, and because He did not need anyone to bear witness concerning man for He Himself knew what was in man. (vv. 23–25)

As Bruce Milne explains, "Jesus of all people will not be misled by outward professions of loyalty which do not involve true repentance and heart commitment. The claim to this knowledge of the human heart echoes Jeremiah 17:10, and is an implicit indicator of deity."[10] Once again, John reinforces his theme of Jesus' deity—separate from us in holiness but close to us through infinite care.

III. Applying the Truth

As we step back from these incidents, we find that Christ is the focal point of them all. In changing the water into wine, Jesus' glory is central. In the cleansing of the temple, it's His holiness and authority. In the raising of the temple, it's His resurrecting power. We, too, need to focus on Jesus. In fact, that's our most desperate need. What a difference this would make in Christianity if Christ's followers were all focused on Him. As A. W. Tozer observed,

> Has it ever occurred to you that one hundred pianos all tuned to the same fork are automatically tuned to each other? They are of one accord by being tuned, not to each other, but to another standard to which each one must individually bow. So one hundred worshippers met together, each one looking away to Christ, are in heart nearer to each other than they could possibly be were they to become "unity" conscious and turn their eyes away from God to strive for closer fellowship. . . . The whole Church of God gains when the members that compose it begin to seek a better and a higher life.[11]

And there is no better or higher life than the one in Jesus Christ.

9. Milne, *The Message of John*, p. 69.

10. Milne, *The Message of John*, p. 70.

11. A. W. Tozer, *The Pursuit of God* (Wheaton, Ill.: Tyndale House Publishers, n.d.), p. 97.

Living Insights

John has shown us that Jesus has the ability to transform, the authority to purify, and the power to transcend death. Which of these aspects of Jesus' nature appeals most to you at this time in your life?

Are there areas where you feel bound by man-made rules and regulations, like the Jews were under the Pharisees' strict interpretation of Moses' Law, that need the touch of Christ's transforming grace? Are you relating with God more by rote than from your heart? Is your life characterized more by the water of duty than the wine of joy? What would you like Christ to transform?

_____

_____

_____

_____

_____

_____

Jesus showed great zeal for His Father's honor in His house, the temple. How passionate are you about God's honor? What do you do that might detract from honoring God? What enhances and reflects His glory? What would you like Jesus to purify and cleanse in you?

_____

_____

_____

_____

_____

_____

Proverbs 14:31 tells us, "He who oppresses the poor reproaches his Maker, But he who is gracious to the needy honors Him." The money-changing and animal-selling systems at the temple deteriorated into corrupt rackets that defrauded the poor. The injustice must have mingled a certain bitterness and cynicism into the worship of those who had been cheated. How can we relate Jesus' actions to the injustice and corruption that harm the poor in our society? What do you think Jesus would have us do?

_____

_____

_____

_____

_____

_____

Jesus' claim to raise the temple in three days points to Himself as the new temple of God, where the Creator and the created can meet heart to heart. It also reveals His resurrection power. Ephesians 1:19–20 tells us that this same power is at work in us and on our behalf. In what areas of your life do you need the touch of Jesus' power?

_____

_____

_____

_____

_____

Jesus knows what is in each of us (John 2:25)—our faults and failures, our darkness and defeat. But He hasn't come merely to point an accusing finger and judge us, as we will see especially clearly in our next chapter. He has come to save, to enlighten, to make us children of God (1:9, 12, 17). So let's entrust ourselves to Him, and let Him transform, cleanse, and bring power to the areas of our lives that need it most.

Chapter 6

Brainstorming the New Birth

John 3:1–21

July 2, 1505. Martin Luther, returning home from a visit with his parents, found himself caught in a violent storm. Terrified, he vowed to become a monk if he were allowed to live.

Luther made it through the storm and fulfilled his vow, entering the Augustinian order of monks in Erfurt, Germany. By his own admission, he entered the monastery more out of constraint than commitment. Reflecting on the incident years later, Luther said: "Not freely or desirously did I become a monk, but walled around with the terror and agony of sudden death, I vowed a constrained and necessary vow."[1]

While at the monastery and as a friar at the University of Wittenberg, Luther diligently, even obsessively, performed his religious tasks. He frequently went to confession and dutifully fulfilled the imposed penances.

But his hard work, his confessions, and his penances never seemed enough. Anguished of soul, Luther wrestled with his own salvation. Hungering for acceptance by God, he realized his emptiness. Gnawing inside was the incessant, ravenous truth that his external righteousness wasn't enough: "For however irreproachably I lived as a monk, I felt myself in the presence of God to be a sinner with a most unquiet conscience, nor could I believe that I pleased him with my satisfactions."[2]

On a trip to Rome, which he thought would earn him some form of spiritual merit, he climbed the steps of Pilate's house on his knees. It is suggested by some church historians that this was where Luther first gained a true understanding of the gospel. As he climbed those stone-hard steps of religious works, a verse came to his mind that changed his life: Romans 1:17, "The righteous man shall live by faith." Like a flash of lightning, the realization struck him: It is *faith* that justifies—not works!

Luther looked back on that revelation as the time of his conversion: "At last I began to understand the justice of God as that by which the just man lives by the gift of God. . . . 'The just man shall live by faith.' At this I felt myself to have been born again, and to have entered through open gates into paradise itself."[3]

---

1. *Encyclopaedia Britannica*, 15th ed., see "Martin Luther."

2. *Encyclopaedia Britannica*, "Martin Luther."

3. *Encyclopaedia Britannica*, "Martin Luther."

Luther had lived a rigorously religious life, pounding on heaven's door in the strength of his own works. Exhausted, he fell to his knees before that door and realized a liberating truth: Christ *Himself* is the door, and it opens to no human effort. Rather, the door swings on the well-oiled hinges of Christ's righteousness and God's grace—and opens only by faith (John 10:9).

I. Contrast: Religion and Regeneration

Religion attempts to turn over new leaves; regeneration transforms lives. Religion is *human effort to reach God*—our attempt to gain God's favor; regeneration is *God's effort to reach us*—His demonstration of love based on grace, aside from any merit on our part. The human plan of salvation involves an external series of good works—church attendance, baptism, giving, benevolent deeds. God's plan is an internal gift from Himself—the impartation of new life by means of a spiritual rebirth. Luther spent years enmeshed in religious works, but it was not until he came to Christ by faith alone that he experienced regeneration.

II. Conversation: Nicodemus and Jesus

"Religious" people are often the most difficult to lead to Christ. They may be brilliant scholars, gifted leaders, or just "good folks," but they can suffer from a blindness that is almost impenetrable. A classic example is found in John 3.

A. Credentials (vv. 1, 10). Nicodemus had an impeccable résumé. If heaven could be earned from one's accomplishments, Nicodemus would have had change left over. In verses 1 and 10, we discover three salient facts about his background: he was "a man of the Pharisees[4] . . . a ruler of the Jews[5] . . . the teacher of Israel."[6]

B. Interchange (vv. 2–15). Undoubtedly, Nicodemus' credentials would have been severely undermined if he were seen with such a renegade as Jesus. Consequently, this renowned religious

---

4. The word *pharisee* comes from a Hebrew root that means "to be separated." Standing aloof from society in self-righteous smugness (compare Luke 18:9–14), these separatist Pharisees were a tight-knit brotherhood dedicated to preserving, interpreting, and defending Jewish Law, which they legalistically forced upon the people of Israel. Commenting on the commandment to keep the Sabbath holy, these theological hair-splitters devoted sixty-four and a half columns in the Jerusalem *Talmud* to Sabbath requirements. They also wrote twenty-four chapters in the *Mishnah* defining what qualified as work on the Sabbath and what didn't. See William Barclay, *The Gospel of John*, rev. ed., The Daily Study Bible Series (Philadelphia, Pa.: Westminster Press, 1975), vol. 1, p. 121.

5. As ruler of the Jews, Nicodemus would have been a member of the Sanhedrin—a court of seventy men who had religious jurisdiction over every Jew in the world.

6. The fact that Jesus acknowledged Nicodemus as *the* teacher of Israel indicates that this religious leader had preeminent status in religious circles and was highly honored.

leader wrapped himself in the cloak of darkness to steal a few furtive moments with this controversial man—the one who changed water into wine and overturned tables in the temple. Perhaps, too, he saw evening as the best time for unhurried, undisturbed conversation. Little did Nicodemus realize, however, that when he met with Jesus, he, the leading teacher of Israel, would be the one raising his hand and asking the elementary-school questions.

1. **Theological discussion** (vv. 2–13). Like a well-volleyed tennis match, an interchange of dialogue bounces back and forth between Nicodemus and Jesus.

> This man came to Him by night, and said to Him, "Rabbi, we know that You have come from God as a teacher; for no one can do these signs that You do unless God is with him." (v. 2)

A high lob by Nicodemus, served politely into Jesus' court. But with a strong, precise shot, Jesus aims the conversation directly at the religious teacher's theological racket.

> "Truly, truly, I say to you, unless one is born again, he cannot see the kingdom of God."[7] (v. 3)

Just as we must experience conception to begin physical, human life, so we must experience a rebirth, or conception from above, to begin spiritual, divine life (compare 1:12–13). But the metaphor catches Nicodemus off guard. Struggling to regain his balance, he backhands a question.

> "How can a man be born when he is old? He cannot enter a second time into his mother's womb and be born, can he?" (v. 4)

Jesus positions Himself center court and answers,

> "Truly, truly, I say to you, unless one is born of water[8] and the Spirit, he cannot enter into the kingdom of God. That which is born of the

---

7. The theme of the dialogue is the new birth. The term "born again," or *gennethei anōthen*, introduced here by Jesus, has never been used in the Bible up to this point. We get our word *regeneration* from the Latin rendering of the phrase "born again." Some scholars translate it as "born from above," focusing on the divine initiative in salvation.

8. The phrase "born of water" is puzzling. Some commentators teach that it refers to baptism; others, to physical birth; others still, to the cleansing work of the Spirit when He comes into a person's life. Three reasons argue for the latter interpretation: (1) water was always used in certain pharisaic rites to symbolize cleansing; (2) because the original Greek uses only the one preposition *of* to govern two objects, neither having a definite article, the translation should read "of water (even) Spirit"; and (3) Titus 3:5 offers a parallel—"He saved us, not on the basis of deeds which we have done in righteousness, but according to His mercy, by the washing of regeneration and renewing by the Holy Spirit."

flesh is flesh, and that which is born of the Spirit is spirit. Do not marvel that I said to you, 'You must be born again.' The wind blows where it wishes and you hear the sound of it, but do not know where it comes from and where it is going; so is everyone who is born of the Spirit." (vv. 5–8)

Nicodemus reaches to return another question.

"How can these things be?" (v. 9)

Jesus fires a power shot over the net, sending it squarely at Nicodemus' tightly strung heart.

"Are you the teacher of Israel, and do not understand these things? Truly, truly, I say to you, we speak that which we know, and bear witness of that which we have seen; and you do not receive our witness. If I told you earthly things and you do not believe, how shall you believe if I tell you heavenly things? And no one has ascended into heaven, but He who descended from heaven, even the Son of Man." (vv. 10–13)

2. **Historical illustration** (vv. 14–15). With a reference to Jewish history, Jesus brings the match to a close. Game: Jesus.

"And as Moses lifted up the serpent in the wilderness, even so must the Son of Man be lifted up; that whoever believes may in Him have eternal life."

A determined teacher, Jesus alludes to a familiar story in Numbers 21:4–9 in an effort to illustrate His point, which still seems hazy to Nicodemus. In the story, Israel was murmuring against the Lord so He sent fiery serpents among them as punishment. The serpents killed a number of people and made many others sick. As a remedy for their sin, God had Moses make a bronze serpent and raise it on a pole for all to see. If the people looked up at the serpent with even a hint of faith in God's provision, they were healed. All this was a striking foreshadowing of Christ being lifted up on the cross to save those who were dying of sin and looked to Him in faith.

A Simple Look of Faith

The Israelites bitten by the serpents needed only to look with faith at God's provision for their sin to be healed.

45

They were not told to concoct some remedy. They were not told to fight the serpents . . . or make an offering . . . or pray . . . or even look to Moses.

All that was required was a simple look of faith on what God provided—like that of the thief on the cross, who merely looked to Jesus and said, "Remember me when You come into Your kingdom!" (Luke 23:42) . . . and the King answered, "Truly I say to you, today you shall be with Me in Paradise" (v. 43).

A simple look of faith—
That's all it took
To exchange a lifelong wilderness of
    shame
For paradise.

III. Clarification: Belief and Unbelief

At this point in the conversation, a footnote is added, the first verse of which has become the most quoted passage in all the Bible.

"For God so loved the world, that He gave His only begotten Son, that whoever believes in Him should not perish, but have eternal life. For God did not send the Son into the world to judge the world, but that the world should be saved through Him. He who believes in Him is not judged; he who does not believe has been judged already, because he has not believed in the name of the only begotten Son of God." (vv. 16–18)

This verbal match between Israel's top-seeded teachers clearly defines the issues. There are only two possible responses to Jesus: belief or unbelief. And there are only two possible destinies to which those responses lead: eternal life . . . or eternal death.

IV. Conclusion: Light and Darkness

Verses 19–21 are a theological postscript, explaining why some believe and others don't.

"And this is the judgment, that the light is come into the world, and men loved the darkness rather than the light; for their deeds were evil. For everyone who does evil hates the light, and does not come to the light, lest his deeds should be exposed. But he who practices the truth comes to the light, that his deeds may be manifested as having been wrought in God."

Ultimately, one's morality *does* influence one's theology. And sometimes to such an extent that many would rather skulk blindly in the dark cave of their sin, awaiting judgment, than bask, forgiven, in the dawn radiating from the true Light of this world.

A Happy Ending

Fortunately, like any good storyteller, John doesn't leave us in the dark regarding the outcome of the encounter between Nicodemus and Jesus. And it's a happy outcome to boot!

After Jesus was crucified, Joseph of Arimathea requested His body from Pilate so he could give his Savior a proper burial. Assisting in the burial was a man who now ventured to be seen with Jesus, fearless and unashamed, in the full light of day.

> And Nicodemus came also, who had first come to Him by night; bringing a mixture of myrrh and aloes, about a hundred pounds weight. And so they took the body of Jesus, and bound it in linen wrappings with the spices, as is the burial custom of the Jews. (19:39–40)

 Living Insights

How could "the teacher of Israel," this Pharisee among Pharisees, this member of the elite Sanhedrin—this supposed Scripture expert—not understand what Jesus was saying about the need to be born again "of water and the Spirit" (John 3:3, 5–6)? Let's take a look at some of the sacred texts he must have passed by.

Look up the following passages, and write down how they could have prepared Nicodemus for what Jesus told him.

Psalm 51:10 _____

_____

Jeremiah 31:31–34 _____

_____

Ezekiel 11:19 _____

_____

Ezekiel 36:25–26 _____

_____

In these passages, who takes the initiative—who provides what we need—God or us?

_____

God has always taken the initiative toward His people, hasn't He? Yet, if we are more focused on working our own way to God, as Nicodemus and the Pharisees were, we will miss what God is doing on our behalf. Instead, we'll institute a judgmental religion, because we will be proud of our own works and look down on others who don't live up to our standards. There's not much room for grace and love in that, is there? Look up the following passages to see the consistency of God's loving initiative toward us.

Exodus 19:4 _____

_____

Deuteronomy 7:6–9 _____

_____

2 Samuel 7 _____

_____

_____

Hosea 2:14–23 _____

_____

_____

As John tells us, Jesus has come to save us, not to judge us; to bring us into the light, not leave us in the dark; to give us eternal life, not to condemn us to everlasting punishment. If you've been depending on your own good works to get you to heaven, you've missed God's message (and heaven too). Trust in His love, won't you? He has provided all you need for eternal life in His Son, Jesus Christ. And it's yours for the taking just by placing your faith in Him, no religious hoops to jump through required.

Chapter 7
The Preacher Who Lost His Congregation
John 3:22–36

"Truly, I say to you, among those born of women there has not arisen anyone greater than John the Baptist." (Matt. 11:11a)

That accolade from Jesus sounds like one that might have been conferred upon Moses, a man handpicked by God to deliver Israel from the Egyptians . . . or upon David, who slew the giant and became the most renowned king in Israel's history.

Instead, those laudatory words fell like garlands around the neck of an unsung hero named John. Unconventional, to say the least, John was an eccentric hermit living in the wilderness, proclaiming an uncompromising message of repentance to prepare the people's hearts for the Messiah.

Clothed in camel hair and a leather belt, he was hardly dressed for success. His Spartan diet of locusts and honey would never have sparked a culinary trend, even among the most austere of nutritionists. And with his abrasive rhetoric, John wouldn't have been a likely choice for any political hopeful's campaign manager.

Yet God appointed this enigma of a man to represent His Son as His forerunner, a job with three primary functions:

- *to clear the way*—to remove obstacles from the minds and hearts of others so they would be ready for the Messiah;

- *to prepare the way*—to promote repentance on the part of the nation so He would be accepted;

- and *to get out of the way*—to step aside once the Messiah had been introduced.

In this lesson, we'll see him getting out of the way . . . probably the toughest part of his job description and, undoubtedly, the reason Jesus called him a great man.

I. Biographical Situation: He Must Increase
Like a small lamp held high in some obscure corner of a dark house, John upheld a solitary wick of testimony about Jesus, the true Light of the World. But as others began to follow him, John became well aware that his ministry and Jesus' had all the potential

for competition. But because the wick was content to serve the Light, any shadows of conflict were quickly dispelled. Watch how a potentially volatile situation arises—and how John humbly handles it.

A. Location of Jesus and John. To begin with, notice that their two ministries were operating on the same turf (compare 3:22 with Matt. 3:1).

> After these things Jesus and His disciples came into the land of Judea, and there He was spending time with them and baptizing.[1] And John also was baptizing in Aenon near Salim, because there was much water there; and they were coming and were being baptized. For John had not yet been thrown into prison. (John 3:22–24)

Jesus' ministry had been in Galilee up to this time. Now He moves into John's domain. Territorial creatures that we are, mere geographical proximity could have created conflict, as it did between the herdsmen of Abram and Lot (see Gen. 13:1–12). In fact, although John wasn't bothered, a little friction from his disciples does begin to heat up the Judean wilderness.

B. Discussion among John's disciples. A man in John's audience, a Jew who had probably heard Jesus' teaching, sparks a debate with a question about ceremonial washing.

> There arose therefore a discussion on the part of John's disciples with a Jew about purification. (v. 25)

The Greek word for *discussion, zētēsis,* means "a searching . . . a dispute." The NIV gets to the heart of the matter with "argument." Because of this verbal confrontation, apparently rooted in whose ways of purification were best—the Jews', John's, or Jesus'—John's disciples come to him, complaining that he is losing some of his flock to this fledgling preacher.

> And they came to John and said to him, "Rabbi, He who was with you beyond the Jordan, to whom you have borne witness, behold, He is baptizing, and all are coming to Him." (v. 26)

"Hey Preacher, you gotta do something! Attendance is way down, and we're losing a lot of members to that new church down the street!" Sound familiar? John's disciples are feeling the crunch of competition. But instead of inventing some glitzy gimmick to recapture the thinning multitudes, John pulls a different strategy out of his camel-hair sleeve.

---

1. The imperfect tense of the verbs in the phrase "was spending time with them and baptizing" indicates that Jesus kept doing this or continued to do so (the same tense is used of John baptizing in v. 23).

C. Reaction of the forerunner. John's response throws cold water on his inflamed disciples, quenching the conversation and their competitive spirit.

> "A man can receive nothing, unless it has been given him from heaven. You yourselves bear me witness, that I said, 'I am not the Christ,' but, 'I have been sent before Him.' He who has the bride is the bridegroom; but the friend of the bridegroom, who stands and hears him, rejoices greatly because of the bridegroom's voice. And so this joy of mine has been made full. He must increase, but I must decrease." (vv. 27–30)

His response incorporates four ideas. First, God is in charge—not people (v. 27). Second, all work is significant—but only one work is preeminent (v. 28). Third, joy comes from being obedient, not from getting glory (v. 29). Fourth, humility calls attention to Christ, not self (v. 30). A similar response can be seen in Moses as he dealt with the competitive spirit that surfaced in his followers regarding two young, upstart prophets.

> But two men had remained in the camp; the name of one was Eldad and the name of the other Medad. And the Spirit rested upon them (now they were among those who had been registered, but had not gone out to the tent), and they prophesied in the camp. So a young man ran and told Moses and said, "Eldad and Medad are prophesying in the camp." Then Joshua the son of Nun, the attendant of Moses from his youth, answered and said, "Moses, my lord, restrain them." But Moses said to him, "Are you jealous for my sake? Would that all the Lord's people were prophets, that the Lord would put His Spirit upon them!" (Num. 11:26–29)

Coping with Envy and Jealousy

"Jealously and envy are often used interchangeably, but there is a difference. Envy begins with empty hands, mourning for what it *doesn't* have. . . . Jealousy is not quite the same. It begins with full hands but is threatened by the loss of its plenty. It is the pain of losing what I have to someone else."[2]

---

2. Charles R. Swindoll, *Killing Giants, Pulling Thorns* (Portland, Ore.: Multnomah Press, 1978), p. 23.

John and Moses certainly knew how to cope with envy and jealousy. So did the psalmist who wrote:

> For not from the east, nor from the west,
> Nor from the desert comes exaltation;
> But God is the Judge;
> He puts down one, and exalts another.
> (Ps. 75:6–7)

Envy often rears its ugly head when one of our peers is promoted . . . when a newcomer passes us on the way up the corporate ladder . . . when we're a senior on the bench and a sophomore is in the starting line-up . . . when a new business sprouts up and over-shadows ours overnight.

Envy's evil twin, jealousy, tags along when loyalties shift . . . when close friends abandon us for others . . . when retirement comes and our authority is handed to a replacement.

Like muggers in a dark alley, envy and jealousy wait to do us in—to rob us of our joy, work us over, and leave our spiritual lives for dead.

Are you going to let that happen to you? The only way to stop it is to walk down another street, the well-lit street of humility—a street illumined not by our own light but by the light of Another, whose sandal we are not worthy to untie.

II. Doctrinal Declaration

In John 3:31–35, our humble forerunner delivers his doctrinal statement on the person of Christ, progressively unfurling a leaf of truth that stems from the prologue in chapter 1.

> "He who comes from above is above all, he who is of the earth is from the earth and speaks of the earth. He who comes from heaven is above all. What He has seen and heard, of that He bears witness; and no man receives His witness. He who has received His witness has set his seal to this, that God is true. For He whom God has sent speaks the words of God; for He gives the Spirit without measure. The Father loves the Son, and has given all things into His hand."

At the end of his message, John gives an altar call that would jostle even the most complacent off the fence.

> "He who believes in the Son has eternal life; but he who does not obey the Son shall not see life, but the wrath of God abides on him." (v. 36)

Moment of Decision

In verse 29, John refers to himself as "the friend of the bridegroom," a rough equivalent to our culture's best man.

According to Jewish tradition, the friend was a liaison between the bride and the bridegroom. He would arrange the details of the wedding—such as sending out invitations, making announcements, and presiding over the marriage feast. His special duty, however, was to guard the bridal chamber.

He would let no one into that chamber except the bride, who secretly slipped away from the celebrating crowd to join the groom. Sometime later, after the union was consummated, the groom came out and announced the fact with a shout. Upon hearing the groom's voice, the friend of the bridegroom would be happy and relieved. His job was done. His joy was full. He could now step out of the way.

John is saying, essentially, "I'm like the friend. I do my task best when I've stepped out of the way."

How about you? Are you content to be the faceless, offstage voice announcing the star of the show? Can you give Jesus center stage while you operate the curtains and unveil Him to the audience? Can you turn the spotlight away from yourself and onto Him?

You can if you become a person like John . . . if you're willing to play a minor part without upstaging the lead and stealing the show yourself.

That will be easy if Jesus is truly *first* in your life. And you can tell whether He is first if you're happy in *second* place, and if you're willing to surrender *any* spotlight to Him.

Living Insights

The application of John the Baptizer's teaching centers on the preeminence of Christ . . . giving Him first place in your life.[3] What does that mean for you?

_____

_____

_____

---

3. This Living Insight has been taken from the original *Exalting Christ . . . the Son of God* study guide (Fullerton, Calif.: Insight for Living, 1987), and was written by Bill Butterworth.

Have you given Him first place? If so, how has your life changed since then?

_____

_____

_____

_____

_____

_____

Was it a one-time decision, or is it a daily one? Why?

_____

_____

_____

_____

_____

What are your biggest struggles in releasing areas of control?

_____

_____

_____

_____

_____

_____

_____

Chapter 8

Water for a Thirsty Woman

John 4:1–42

In this next chapter of John's Gospel, we'll see Jesus offering living water to a sun-parched woman at a Samaritan well—water that all humanity thirsts for. Professor Zane Hodges discusses this longing in his excellent book *The Hungry Inherit.*

> Love, success, wealth, fame—these were but a few of the countless springs at which men had stooped to drink, only to rise from them to find that they offered no lasting inward satisfaction, no enduring personal fulfillment. . . .
>
> But His water was different! It could accomplish a miracle! The one who drank it was secure from thirst, not merely for time but for eternity as well. . . . So vital, so transforming was such a drink, that in the innermost being of the man who drank it, there was created an inexhaustible fountain of life. The waters of that hidden inner spring could not run dry; they could not be stanched; they virtually leaped up to produce the surpassing experience of eternal life.[1]

Such was the experience of the Samaritan woman in John 4, and such is the offer to all who come to Christ. With one sip of faith, our deepest thirst is quenched. And what was once a wilderness of wants is transformed into an oasis overflowing with abundant life.

Journeying back through the years of time, let's stop now and rest at the well where that offer was first made.

I. The Setting

In verses 1–2, we find the Pharisees getting wind of Jesus' rising popularity. When Jesus realizes this, He takes His disciples and leaves Judea for Galilee (v. 3). En route, He passes through Samaria (v. 4). Exhausted by the long trip, He comes to rest at a well outside the town of Sychar—Jacob's well, to be exact (vv. 5–6). It is the sixth hour of the day, just about noon, and the impartial Palestinian sun beats down on this tired traveler. His hungry disciples, meanwhile, have gone ahead into the city for food. As His weary, waiting eyes scan the horizon, His unsuspecting appointment arrives, carrying a water pot on her head.

---

1. Zane Clark Hodges, *The Hungry Inherit* (Chicago, Ill.: Moody Press, 1972), pp. 13–14.

II. The Conversation

In those days, women normally drew water at dawn or dusk, the cooler hours of the day. It was a time to visit, to exchange news, to idle away a little time gossiping. That this woman has come to the well at noon, the hottest hour of the day, hints at her reputation (compare vv. 18 and 28). Promiscuous with the men and, consequently, cold-shouldered by the women, she braves the brazen sun to avoid the searing stares of the more reputable.

A. **The discussion** (vv. 7–26). The woman comes bearing a dry, empty pot, a telling symbol of her parched, barren heart. Jesus opens the conversation with a direct, and somewhat disarming, request, "Give Me a drink" (v. 7). But she responds defensively to His simple petition.

> How is it that You, being a Jew, ask me for a drink since I am a Samaritan woman? (For Jews have no dealings with Samaritans.) (v. 9)

Intense racial hatred existed between Jews and Samaritans, much of it centering on religious differences.[2] So great was this animosity that, in traveling from Judea to Galilee, Jews would go miles out of their way to avoid crossing the Samaritan border.[3] And not only is our noonday patron of the well a Samaritan—she is a woman. Cultural sentiment for women was extremely low during the time of Christ. The Pharisees taught that men should not speak to women in public.[4] Some men were even so rigid as to refuse to look at a woman they passed on the street. But Christ not only looks at her and speaks with her, He does so kindly and in such a way as to whet her appetite for spiritual things.

> Jesus answered and said to her, "If you knew the gift of God, and who it is who says to you, 'Give Me a drink,' you would have asked Him, and He would have given you living water." (v. 10)

2. For example, the Samaritans had as their Scripture the five books of Moses—Genesis through Deuteronomy. The Jews, having the entire Old Testament as their Scripture, looked down on the religion of the Samaritans as impoverished and incomplete. For more information on the rift between the Jews and Samaritans, consult Leon Morris' *The Word Was Made Flesh: John 1–5*, vol. 1 of *Reflections on the Gospel of John* (Grand Rapids, Mich.: Baker Book House, 1986), pp. 120–23.

3. For strict Jews, the route for travel from Jerusalem to Galilee lay through the region beyond the Jordan. The shortcut through Samaria was used only by those in a hurry.

4. Leon Morris quotes the rabbinic attitude toward women at the time of Christ: "He that talks much with womankind brings evil upon himself and neglects the study of the Law." One of the Jewish prayers included the phrase, "Blessed art thou, O Lord . . . who hast not made me a woman." *The Gospel according to John*, rev. ed., The New International Commentary on the New Testament Series (Grand Rapids, Mich.: William B. Eerdmans Publishing Co., 1995), pp. 242–43, n. 67.

But His alluring conversation is met with skepticism and sarcasm.

> She said to Him, "Sir, You have nothing to draw with
> and the well is deep; where then do You get that
> living water? You are not greater than our father
> Jacob, are You, who gave us the well, and drank of
> it himself, and his sons, and his cattle?" (vv. 11–12)

With her who-do-you-think-you-are question, she makes a mild attempt at putting Jesus in His place. But Jesus responds by patiently appealing to her immediate desire for physical water. And, in doing so, He appeals to her greater, though less obvious, spiritual thirst.

> Jesus answered and said to her, "Everyone who
> drinks of this water shall thirst again; but whoever
> drinks of the water that I shall give him shall never
> thirst; but the water that I shall give him shall be-
> come in him a well of water springing up to eternal
> life." (vv. 13–14)

Seeing only from a human viewpoint, however, the woman misses His point entirely.

> The woman said to Him, "Sir, give me this water, so
> I will not be thirsty, nor come all the way here to
> draw." (v. 15)

Feeling that the conversation is beginning to meander down a dead-end path, Jesus points to her personal life. In effect, He places a full-length mirror in front of her, forcing her to take a good, hard look at herself.

> He said to her, "Go, call your husband, and come
> here." (v. 16)

Like the sobering reflection that greets you when you first wake up, this woman's glimpse of herself makes her flush with embarrassment. But when she tries to skirt the mirrored issues, Jesus nudges her into facing the emptiness within her heart.

> The woman answered and said, "I have no hus-
> band." Jesus said to her, "You have well said, 'I have
> no husband'; for you have had five husbands, and
> the one whom you now have is not your husband;
> this you have said truly." (vv. 17–18)

Christ's sharp perception pricks her conscience, and the desolation and shame is more than she can bear. Squirming, she shifts to more comfortable conversation.

> "Sir, I perceive that You are a prophet. Our fathers
> worshiped in this mountain, and you people say

that in Jerusalem is the place where men ought to worship." (vv. 19–20)

What about the unsaved in Africa? How can a good God allow suffering and evil? What about creation and evolution? Sprinkling or immersion . . . wine or grape juice . . . King James or Living Bible? Distracting questions about religious peripherals. This is the smoke screen she hopes will hide her blemished soul from the dawning light of His penetrating gaze. But it is no use. A radiant shaft of truth pierces the veil.

> Jesus said to her, "Woman, believe Me, an hour is coming when neither in this mountain, nor in Jerusalem, shall you worship the Father. You worship that which you do not know; we worship that which we know, for salvation is from the Jews. But an hour is coming, and now is, when the true worshipers shall worship the Father in spirit and truth; for such people the Father seeks to be His worshipers. God is spirit, and those who worship Him must worship in spirit and truth." (vv. 21–24)

He clears away the mist: it is not *where* one worships that matters; it is *how* and, ultimately, *who* one worships that are important. Jesus brings the conversation to such a burning focus that her very soul is on the verge of igniting.

> The woman said to Him, "I know that Messiah is coming (He who is called Christ); when that One comes, He will declare all things to us." (v. 25)

B. The declaration (v. 26). A foreigner, a Samaritan, a woman, and, to top it all off, a woman of low morals and ill repute. To a strict Jew, she is indeed far from the kingdom of God. But because of a man she knows simply as "a Jew" (v. 9) . . . then as "Sir" (vv. 11, 15) . . . then as "a prophet" (v. 19), she now crouches on the brink of total acceptance, waiting to make that leap of faith—somewhat fearfully, but most certainly—as she listens with piqued interest for the revealing of this mysterious visitor's true identity.

> Jesus said to her, "I who speak to you am He." (v. 26)

III. The Reaction

Just at that dramatic, cliff-hanging moment, guess who shows up with the burgers and fries? The disciples. It's an awkward situation for everyone—everyone, that is, except Jesus.

> And at this point His disciples came, and they marveled that He had been speaking with a woman; yet no one said, "What do You seek?" or, "Why do You speak with her?" (v. 27)

A. Of the Samaritan woman.

So the woman left her water pot, and went into the city, and said to the men, "Come, see a man who told me all the things that I have done; this is not the Christ, is it?" (vv. 28–29)

The Moment of Faith

"Like the sun bursting forth from behind the clouds, the light of truth had flooded her soul. She turned from Him, the water jar she had come to fill standing empty upon the ground, but the heart she had not come to fill now overflowing with living water."[5]

Just as Jesus had earlier turned ordinary water into the most festive of wines, He now takes the emptiest of lives and fills it full.

He can do that with your life too. No matter how stagnant the water . . . no matter how empty the pot.

All it takes is a sip of faith.

B. Of the Samaritan men.
Like a stone plopped into water, Jesus' words of life fall into the Samaritan woman's heart and then ripple through the city. The response to this one changed life is overwhelming. Swells of people flow from the city and pour over the countryside on their way to Jesus.

They went out of the city, and were coming to Him.
. . .
And from that city many of the Samaritans believed in Him because of the word of the woman who testified, "He told me all the things that I have done." So when the Samaritans came to Him, they were asking Him to stay with them; and He stayed there two days. And many more believed because of His word; and they were saying to the woman, "It is no longer because of what you said that we believe, for we have heard for ourselves and know that this One is indeed the Savior of the world." (vv. 30, 39–42)

A solitary seed has been planted, and within the time it takes to eat lunch, an entire field of humanity becomes ripe for harvest for the kingdom of God.

---

5. Hodges, *The Hungry Inherit*, p. 18.

C. Of the disciples. Meanwhile, the disciples have their minds on a more pressing matter—food!

> The disciples were requesting Him, saying, "Rabbi, eat." But He said to them, "I have food to eat that you do not know about." The disciples therefore were saying to one another, "No one brought Him anything to eat, did he?" (vv. 31–33)

While they're preoccupied with passing the salt and catsup, Jesus teaches them a vital lesson about another kind of food.

> "My food is to do the will of Him who sent Me, and to accomplish His work. Do you not say, 'There are yet four months, and then comes the harvest'? Behold, I say to you, lift up your eyes, and look on the fields, that they are white for harvest. Already he who reaps is receiving wages, and is gathering fruit for life eternal; that he who sows and he who reaps may rejoice together. For in this case the saying is true, 'One sows, and another reaps.' I sent you to reap that for which you have not labored; others have labored, and you have entered into their labor." (vv. 34–38)

A Concluding Application

The Samaritan woman needed water. But the disciples, whose thirst had already been quenched by the river of life, needed food.

A sinner's greatest need is the free gift of salvation. The greatest need of one who is saved is to understand and do the will of God.

For you who are empty and don't know Jesus personally, like the Samaritan woman—you are offered the incredible gift of eternal life. For you whom Jesus has already brought into His family, like the disciples—you are given the incomparable offer to work with Him side by side, receiving the laborer's reward and sharing in the joy of the harvest.

What an incredible and incomparable Savior, who not only gives us the grace to receive Him but also the dignity of serving with Him in ripened fields (Eph. 2:8–10).

Living Insights

In the prejudiced society of first-century Palestine, few people were valued less in the system than a Samaritan woman—especially one with loose morals. It would have been easy for Jesus to pass right by her, to pretend He didn't see her, to not acknowledge her existence. But He didn't do that.

He looked at her, read her circumstances, felt the need of her heart. He engaged her, treating her not as a problem to be solved but as one who has something to offer (John 4:7). He listened to her, didn't argue with her, didn't shame her. He wasn't out to win a debate; He wanted to win her soul (vv. 26, 36). This is truly the Father's work, isn't it (v. 34)?

How well are you doing at the Father's work? How do you feel about and treat the marginalized in your society—the homeless, the poor, the person of a different color or nationality from you, the person with AIDS, the prisoner? Are you pretending not to see them, or are you seeing the eternal soul within each one?

_____

_____

_____

_____

_____

_____

Do you sometimes struggle to personally reach out to them? If so, why? Perhaps it's fear blocking you, or the social stigma that person carries, or judgmentalism, or complacency, or maybe just not knowing what to do. What do you think it might be for you?

_____

_____

_____

_____

_____

Reread Jesus' exchange with the Samaritan woman in John 4. In what ways would you like to be more like Christ in your dealings with other people?

_____

_____

_____

_____

_____

_____

_____

_____

When we treat the people of God's creation with honor, kindness, and care for their redemption—isn't that a crucial part of worshiping God "in spirit and truth" (vv. 23–24)?

"But when the Son of Man comes in His glory, and all the angels with Him, then He will sit on His glorious throne. And all the nations will be gathered before Him; and He will separate them from one another, as the shepherd separates the sheep from the goats; and He will put the sheep on His right, and the goats on the left. Then the King will say to those on His right, 'Come, you who are blessed of My Father, inherit the kingdom prepared for you from the foundation of the word. For I was hungry, and you gave Me something to eat; I was thirsty, and you gave Me drink; I was a stranger, and you invited Me in; naked, and you clothed Me; I was sick, and you visited Me; I was in prison, and you came to Me. . . . Truly I say to you, to the extent that you did it to one of these brothers of Mine, even the least of them, you did it to Me.'" (Matt. 25:31–36, 40)

Chapter 9

Healing at a Distance

John 4:46–54

Most Americans can expect to live about seventy years, according to statistics. But the statistical tables don't always work out with real-life precision. For example, we expect to face the deaths of our parents someday. We don't expect, however, to face the deaths of our children.

Nicholas Wolterstorff certainly didn't. But one bright Sunday afternoon, a numbing telephone call brought news of a mountain-climbing accident. In his book *Lament for a Son*, the bereaved father reflects upon the painful loss of his son.

> Gone from the face of the earth. I wait for a group of students to cross the street, and suddenly I think: He is not there. I go to a ball game and find myself singling out the twenty-five-year olds; none of them is he. In all the crowds and streets and rooms and churches and schools and libraries and gatherings of friends in our world, on all the mountains, I will not find him. Only his absence.
>
> Silence. "Was there a letter from Eric today?" "When did Eric say he would call?" Now only silence. Absence and silence.
>
> When we gather now there's always someone missing, his absence as present as our presence, his silence as loud as our speech. Still five children, but one always gone.
>
> When we're all together, we're not all together.
>
> It's the *neverness* that is so painful. *Never again* to be here with us—never to sit with us at table, never to travel with us, never to laugh with us, never to cry with us, never to embrace us as he leaves for school, never to see his brothers and sister marry. All the rest of our lives we must live without him.[1]

As we turn to our lesson in John 4, the emotion of another father who fears the death of his son bleeds through the page.

I. The Occasion

The first miracle Jesus performed was the turning of water into wine at the wedding feast in Cana (2:11). In chapter 4, verses 46–54, John records a second miracle—the healing of a government official's son who lay sick some twenty miles away. Two major characters

1. Nicholas Wolterstorff, *Lament for a Son* (Grand Rapids, Mich.: William B. Eerdmans Publishing Co., 1987), pp. 14–15.

enact this emotionally charged drama: Jesus and the royal official. The word translated "royal official" is *basilikos*, and it could be rendered "king's man." Obviously a person of prestigious rank, this man is probably one of Herod's trusted officers. But his rank means nothing to him now. His son's life is at stake. Consequently, he doesn't go to Herod; he goes to Jesus, the very source of life. Amazing, isn't it, how infirmity draws people to Christ faster than prosperity does. But sometimes that's what it takes. As C. S. Lewis observed: "How hard it is to turn our thoughts to God when everything is going well with us."[2]

II. The Conversation

Cupping our ears to overhear the conversation between the royal official and Jesus, we can't help but empathize with this troubled father.

> There was a certain royal official, whose son was sick at Capernaum. When he heard that Jesus had come out of Judea into Galilee, he went to Him, and was requesting Him to come down and heal his son; for he was at the point of death. (vv. 46b–47)

The imperfect tense of the verb *requesting* gives the nuance of continuous action. It could be paraphrased "he kept on begging Him over and over again." Like so many of Christ's followers, the official thought Jesus had to be right by his son's bedside to effectively handle the situation. Although we can understand his urgency, we shouldn't overlook two matters: (1) he told Christ how to handle the need, and (2) he presented the need before presenting himself. How much better it would have been for him to simply lay himself and his problem at the feet of Christ and allow Jesus to handle it *His* way. As we listen to Jesus' response, we might feel, at first glance, that He comes down awfully hard on this desperate father.

> Jesus therefore said to him, "Unless you people see signs and wonders, you simply will not believe." (v. 48)

Before we judge Jesus' words too harshly, we must understand that a circus atmosphere was developing around Christ. To many people, He was fast becoming a traveling sideshow—"Come one, come all! See the Galilean Miracle Worker!" No doubt tearful by now, the broken father persisted. And the persistence of this royal official won him a hearing before the true King.

> The royal official said to Him, "Sir, come down before my child dies." Jesus said to him, "Go your way; your son lives." The man believed the word that Jesus spoke to him, and he started off. (vv. 49–50)

---

2. C. S. Lewis, *The Problem of Pain* (New York, N.Y.: The Macmillan Co., 1962), p. 96.

But why didn't Jesus go to Capernaum Himself? Probably, He wanted to stretch the faith of this official. Standing by and watching as another brings healing requires little faith. But to believe without being there, without seeing for yourself—that takes faith!

Time to Smell the Flowers

We tend to envision long, full lives for all of our children. We forget, though, that the first grave dug was for a son, not a father (Gen. 4:1–11).

Like a blooming orchard caught in an untimely frost, the fruit of the womb is sometimes nipped coldly in the bud.

If you have a blossoming family, now is the time to treasure its fragrance—every unique flower, each individual petal—for you never know if the weather might turn suddenly cold.

III. The Reaction

A. **The official: belief.** The royal official followed Jesus' instructions to be on his way. At first glance, we might assume that he was hurrying back to Capernaum. But the Greek verb for "started off"—*poreuō*—simply means "to go one's way." All we can infer is that he left Jesus' presence absolutely assured that His words formed a promise. And in that promise, he rested. Most likely, he stayed in Cana and went about the business he was there for. Verses 51–52 support that speculation.

> And as he was now going down, his slaves met him, saying that his son was living. So he inquired of them the hour when he began to get better. They said therefore to him, "Yesterday at the seventh hour the fever left him."

Remember now, the towns were no more than twenty miles apart—for a man in a hurry, no more than a four- to five-hour walk. If the healing took place at the seventh hour of the day, or 1:00 P.M., the official could have been home well before nightfall. But note how his servants greet him on the road: "Yesterday . . . " The man must have placed such confidence in Jesus' promise that he didn't return home until the next day. That's faith!

B. **The slaves: excitement.** The imperfect tense of the verb *saying* in verse 51 indicates continual action. Apparently, the slaves were jumping up and down with joy, repeating over and over: "Your son's alive . . . he's living . . . he's well!"

C. The household: revival. The healing not only caused enthusiasm on the road, it created a revival at home.

> So the father knew that it was at that hour in which Jesus said to him, "Your son lives"; and he himself believed, and his whole household. (v. 53)

An interesting possibility related to this story is found in Luke 8:1–3.

> And it came about soon afterwards, that He began going about from one city and village to another, proclaiming and preaching the kingdom of God; and the twelve were with Him, and also some women who had been healed of evil spirits and sicknesses: Mary who was called Magdalene, from whom seven demons had gone out, *and Joanna the wife of Chuza, Herod's steward,* and Susanna, and many others who were contributing to their support out of their private means. (emphasis added)

Look closely at verse 3. Joanna was the wife of Chuza, Herod's steward, who was in charge of the king's financial books—a close, trusted official. He and his wife supported Jesus out of their private means. Possibly, Chuza and Joanna were the grateful parents of the young man healed in John 4.

IV. Conclusion

John concludes the story of the royal official's son with an editorial comment found in verse 54.

> This is again a second sign that Jesus performed, when He had come out of Judea into Galilee.

This statement directly ties in with John's major purpose in writing the book, that the reader might "believe that Jesus is the Christ" (20:31).

V. Application

This moving account of Christ's compassion dramatically illustrates His lordship, not only over the physical realm with regard to sickness, but over the spatial realm as well, as His power to heal spanned a distance of twenty miles. We can also take from this story some lessons on faith's role in parenting—especially you dads.

A. A faithful father isn't too independent to admit his needs (4:46–49). This father sought help when faced with a critical situation. He wasn't afraid to admit his own inadequacy or to ask for help publicly. He didn't pretend to be a stoic pillar of independent strength. How vulnerable are you? How honest are you about your needs . . . with yourself? With God? With your wife? With others?

B. A faithful father isn't too busy to know his children. This father didn't send his wife—"Honey, you take care of it; I've got a lot of work stacked up at the royal office." He went himself. He was involved in his home. Men, do you delegate too much family responsibility to your wife? If you do, she may find it hard to believe you really care.

C. A faithful father isn't too proud to believe God's Word (vv. 50, 53). Maybe, at this very moment, you are separated by distance from a situation you are concerned about. Will you trust God to be there? Will you take Him at His Word? Maybe God has you waiting . . . flat on your back or away from home . . . forcing you to believe Him.

D. A faithful father isn't too logical to walk by faith. Are you a pacesetter in spiritual things? When the members of your family need counsel, do they turn to you? Do you promote Christian activities or are you a barrier to them? If God were to take you this afternoon, would your joyful, free life of faith be what your family remembers most about you?

E. A faithful father isn't too serious to enjoy life with his family. A painful moment of honesty, please. Is this you? "You kids shut up! . . . Turn out those lights. . . . Get that room cleaned up. . . . It costs too much. You think money grows on trees?" God didn't create you to be a sergeant, or the home to be a boot camp, or your children to be Marine Corps recruits. He gave you a family to nurture . . . as a gardener nurtures his plants.

> How blessed is everyone who fears the Lord,
> Who walks in His ways.
> When you shall eat of the fruit of your hands,
> You will be happy and it will be well with you.
> Your wife shall be like a fruitful vine,
> Within your house,
> Your children like olive plants
> Around your table.
> Behold, for thus shall the man be blessed
> Who fears the Lord. (Ps. 128:1–4)

And God gave you a family not only to nurture but to enjoy as well. Will your children remember their childhood as being fun . . . or frantic? The world outside your front door is cold enough. But when the fire flickers out at home . . . how great is the darkness, how piercing the cold.

Jesus chose Cana to be a place of transformations, didn't He? First He changed water into wine, and then He changed a deadly illness into restored life. If we look deeper, we'll see that Jesus' first sign was really about changing the emptiness of law-keeping into the full joy of grace. And His second sign was more about the transformation from spiritual death to spiritual life. For not only was the boy's earthly life restored, but the whole household—family and servants—believed in Jesus and received eternal life.

Jesus cares so much about our faith. That's why He would say with a sigh, "Unless you people see signs and wonders, you simply will not believe" (John 4:48). A faith that depends on miracles can't endure tough times; it's fickle, ebbing and flowing with each desired result we receive or don't receive. It's not the kind of settled, steadfast faith that can trust the Lord when things don't turn out the way we want them to, that can hold on with eyes focused on eternal life.

Signs and wonders may be a good place to begin seeing the Lord's power, but our faith needs to mature into a trust of God's Word and a sure belief in His Person.

How is your faith faring in the midst of life's painful challenges? Have you ever desperately begged Jesus for a miracle? What happened?

_____

_____

_____

_____

_____

_____

If God chose to not miraculously intervene in your situation, how did your faith come through?

_____

_____

_____

_____

_____

_____

_____

One of the beautiful attributes of God is His patience. David reminds us in Psalm 103: "The Lord is compassionate and gracious, Slow to anger and abounding in lovingkindness. . . . For He Himself knows our frame; He is mindful that we are but dust" (vv. 8, 14). And Jesus Himself gave the father in John 4 the opportunity to build his faith in Him by taking Him at His word instead of merely seeing a sign (vv. 49–50). If your faith was pounded against the rocks by the waves of pain, how have you seen the Lord patiently help you rebuild your trust in Him?

_____

_____

_____

_____

_____

_____

Because Jesus wants us with Him in heaven for all eternity (14:1–3), the maturing of our faith is "more precious than gold" to Him (1 Pet. 1:7). Like the father in John 4, let's move beyond a faith that depends on getting our prayers answered the way we want them to and instead anchor our trust in the unseen promises of God and in the One who answers our prayers with our best interest in view.

Chapter 10
An Exposé of Legalism
John 5:1–18

"Thou shalt."
"Thou shalt not."
"Thou shalt!"
"Shalt not!"
"Shalt!"
"Not!"
"SHALT!"
"NOT!"

Sounds like angry children arguing on the playground, doesn't it? But what you're hearing is the insistent bickering of adult Christians entrenched in legalism.

Legalists measure spiritual growth against a yardstick notched incrementally by good works. Like rigid grade-school teachers, they rap their students' knuckles when they don't measure up.

These human standards may conveniently size people up, but in the end, they stunt growth instead of foster it.

The Pharisees are the grandfathers of legalism, and in our Scripture passage today, Jesus meets them in a head-to-head, toe-to-toe confrontation that turns the tide of official opinion against Him.

I. Legalism—Let's Understand It
When we lift the veil on legalism, we find hypocrisy instead of holiness. Let's take a closer look and expose it for the whitewashed tomb it is.

A. What is it? Legalism is conforming to a code of behavior for the purpose of exalting self. Legalists make lists of dos and don'ts based not on Scripture but on tradition or personal preference—then they judge themselves and others on their performance. In a nutshell, it's "checklist Christianity."

B. How does it happen? Legalism slips unnoticed into the church like a deadly enemy cloaked in pious, religious garb. When it does, the Bridegroom's party grows suddenly silent . . . the wine turns quickly back to water . . . and joy in the Christian life soon dries up. The human spirit withers under the critical glare of the legalist. Legalists prey especially on young, biblically naive believers. Paul describes legalists in Galatians 2:4 as "false brethren who had sneaked in to spy out our liberty which we have in Christ Jesus, in order to bring us into bondage."

C. **Why is it wrong?** First and foremost, legalism is unbiblical. Grace and freedom are the hallmarks of the Christian life (John 8:32; Rom. 8:1–4; Gal. 5:1; Eph. 2:4–9), not law and bondage (Gal. 3). Second, it promotes the flesh, which cannot please God (Rom. 8:8). Third, it is based on pride (see Luke 18:9–14). Like an ornate Corinthian column in the temple where the Pharisee prayed, a proud, erect **"I"** is the pillar that supports legalism.

— A Balanced Perspective ————————————

Law and grace are opposite living standards. But this does not mean that there was no grace for those who lived under the Law (see Pss. 51; 103) . . . nor that there are no laws for us, who live under grace (see Rom. 13:8–10; Gal. 6:2; James 1:25; 2:8).

Grace never promotes a do-as-you-please philosophy or a loose life of selfishness, sinfulness, and licentiousness. Romans 6:12–18 confirms this fact (see also Gal. 5:13–14). The major differences, however, between living under the Law and living under grace lie with the recipients of the commands and their motivation to obey.

The Israelites received the Mosaic Law and its more than six hundred commands. They were motivated to obey by *fear* and empowered only by the *flesh*. Today, believers in Jesus Christ receive grace. Although the New Testament also contains hundreds of commands, we are motivated by *love* and empowered by the *Holy Spirit*.

What motivates your obedience to Christ—law and fear, or the grace and love now offered us?

D. **When did it start?** Legalism is an ancient art, perfected by the Pharisees and implemented by subsequent generations of apprentices who have been narrow, rigid, and often intolerably religious. Legalists have refused to accept the doctrine of sheer grace. Instead, they have sought to supplement grace with the mingled alloy of their own works. To this day, pockets of legalism thrive in every corner of the country and in almost every church.

II. Legalism: Let's Examine It

The pivotal issue on which the controversy in John 5 turns is the question of observing the Sabbath. Before we get into that passage, let's do a little spadework to uncover the Sabbath's biblical and traditional roots.

A. Background information. Three pieces of history shed considerable light on the Sabbath and what it means.

    1. Origin of the Sabbath. At the end of Genesis 1, we read that God completed His work of creation in six days. In 2:2, Moses states: "And by the seventh day God completed His work which He had done; and He rested. . . ." Essentially, *sabbath* means rest, translated from the Hebrew term *shabbath.*

    2. Law of the Sabbath. In Exodus 20, the Law God gave to Moses required observance of the Sabbath, and He based His injunction on the pattern of the creation.

> "Remember the sabbath day, to keep it holy. Six days you shall labor and do all your work, but the seventh day is a sabbath of the Lord your God; in it you shall not do any work, you or your son or your daughter, your male or your female servant or your cattle or your sojourner who stays with you. For in six days the Lord made the heavens and the earth, the sea and all that is in them, and rested on the seventh day; therefore the Lord blessed the sabbath day and made it holy." (vv. 8–11)

    3. Tradition of the Sabbath. Slipping in between the Old and New Testaments, the Pharisees amplified the Sabbath law by adding thirty-nine categories of unpermitted work, along with a number of tedious restrictions. These became part of the traditional teachings of the rabbis, who then enforced them among the people. Yet these requirements stretched considerably beyond God's original intent. For example, notice how obsessive the restrictions had become in just this one regulation.

> If a man removed his finger-nails by means of his nails or his teeth, and so, too, if [he pulled out] the hair of his head, or his moustache or his beard; and so, too, if a woman dressed her hair or painted her eyelids or reddened [her face]—such a one [Rabbi] Eliezer declares liable [to a Sin-offering]. (Shab. 10:6)[1]

So much for men biting their nails or women fixing their hair on the way to the synagogue!

---

1. *The Mishnah*, trans. Herbert Danby (Oxford, England: Oxford University Press, 1933), p. 110.

B. Biblical exposition. Now that we understand the Pharisees' legalistic view of the Sabbath, let's turn to a story in John 5 that shows how they valued their traditional principles more than people.

1. The need (vv. 1–5). The opening scene is piercing, even depressing.

> After these things there was a feast of the Jews, and Jesus went up to Jerusalem. Now there is in Jerusalem by the sheep gate a pool, which is called in Hebrew Bethesda, having five porticoes. In these lay a multitude of those who were sick, blind, lame, and withered, [waiting for the moving of the waters; for an angel of the Lord went down at certain seasons into the pool, and stirred up the water; whoever then first, after the stirring up of the water, stepped in was made well from whatever disease with which he was afflicted.] And a certain man was there, who had been thirty-eight years in his sickness.

For thirty-eight years, this pathetic, bruised reed of a man has lain here in poverty and despair. Yet within him flickers a dimly burning wick of hope.

2. The miracle (vv. 6–9a). It was just such bruised reeds and dimly burning wicks that Jesus came to help and to heal (see Isa. 42:1–3). With the tender compassion of a child choosing the runt of the litter, Jesus gives special attention to this withered man.

> When Jesus saw him lying there, and knew that he had already been a long time in that condition, He said to him, "Do you wish to get well?" The sick man answered Him, "Sir, I have no man to put me into the pool when the water is stirred up, but while I am coming, another steps down before me." Jesus said to him, "Arise, take up your pallet, and walk." And immediately the man became well, and took up his pallet and began to walk.

Walking Away from Bethesda

Just as distance was no barrier to healing the royal official's son, so time was no obstacle for Jesus to overcome in healing the lame man. Thirty-eight years of misery, shame, embarrassment, and despair

> . . . in a split second, that was all history.
>
> No matter how miserable your life has been—no matter how lame your spiritual life or how long you've been limping—Jesus can change it. The real question is: Do you wish to get well?
>
> It's easy to become accustomed to life around the pool of misery. The peer group there certainly won't criticize you. People will make space for your pallet and then leave you to yourself—or even commiserate with you.
>
> But maybe, after years of inner poverty, you're looking for a change, longing to be restored to everything God created you to be. If so, Jesus is the ticket out of that slum. If you *really* want to get well, He'll give you the grace and strength to take up your pallet and walk.

3. **The confrontation** (vv. 9b–17). Notice how quickly this sunny moment of joy is muted by the gray shadows of legalism.

> Now it was the Sabbath on that day. Therefore the Jews were saying to him who was cured, "It is the Sabbath, and it is not permissible for you to carry your pallet." (vv. 9b–10)

Undoubtedly, the witnesses around the pool are bustling with excitement. But the miracle leaves the legalists bristling with anger. When they should have been on their knees in praise, the only thing these Pharisees can do is pull out their principle-book and quote condemnation, chapter and verse. And in the midst of their straining the gnat from their list of pure regulations, Jesus slips through the sieve.

> But [the man] answered them, "He who made me well was the one who said to me, 'Take up your pallet and walk.'" They asked him, "Who is the man who said to you, 'Take up your pallet, and walk'?" But he who was healed did not know who it was; for Jesus had slipped away while there was a crowd in that place. Afterward Jesus found him in the temple, and said to him, "Behold, you have become well; do not sin anymore, so that nothing worse

may befall you." The man went away, and told the Jews that it was Jesus who had made him well. And for this reason the Jews were persecuting Jesus, because He was doing these things on the Sabbath. But He answered them, "My Father is working until now, and I Myself am working." (vv. 11–17)

4. The reaction (v. 18). When the Jews hear of Jesus' escape and His testimony to the healed man, they are livid.

For this cause therefore the Jews were seeking all the more to kill Him, because He not only was breaking the Sabbath, but also was calling God His own Father, making Himself equal with God. (v. 18)

Essentially, the indictments of the legalists were twofold: one, Jesus broke the Sabbath (vv. 16, 18); two, Jesus claimed equality with God by claiming Him as His Father (vv. 17–18). Ironically, the Pharisees were the guilty ones: they judged Jesus, refused to rejoice or give praise at the healing, and even went so far as to plot Christ's assassination.

III. Legalism: Let's Avoid It

We must keep legalism from gaining a foothold in our lives and churches. To oppose legalism, *truth* must emerge. Paul confronted legalism, refusing to look the other way (see Gal. 2:14; 4:16). To combat legalism, *conviction* must be employed. This may even mean taking a stand with a good friend or a spiritual leader, as Paul did with Peter when that church rock began to crumble under legalism's heavy weight (see 2:11–14). To overcome legalism, *grace* must be embraced. Works and our obsequious duty to them will never be abandoned until we reach out for God's grace—and as we do, the shackles of legalism will fall from our wrists and ankles. Then and only then will we be truly free.

"For through the Law I died to the Law, that I might live to God. I have been crucified with Christ; and it is no longer I who live, but Christ lives in me; and the life which I now live in the flesh I live by faith in the Son of God, who loved me, and delivered Himself up for me." (Gal. 2:19–20)

☀ Living Insights

"Do you wish to get well?" Jesus asks (John 5:6). That's an intriguing question, isn't it? To some extent, we're all emotionally and spiritually ailing, blind, weak, withered, even paralyzed. But do we want to get well?

If you were lying by that pool in Bethesda, what would be your ailment? What would your condition look like?

_____

_____

_____

_____

_____

_____

_____

Have you had this for a long time? Is it recurring, or is it pretty much constant?

_____

_____

_____

_____

_____

_____

How have you dealt with it? Do you recognize your need? Have you struggled for ages to find healing? Have you waited for someone else to take care of you? Have you become comfortable with your dysfunctions and sins? How would you respond to Jesus' question?

_____

_____

_____

_____

_____

_____

_____

_____

_____

The Pharisees were so blind to their faults that they weren't even aware that they needed healing. That's what legalism does; it blinds us to our own needs and exaggerates others' flaws—both real and imagined. The legalist doesn't realize that we all lie helpless and desperate beside the same pool. And how can we be healed if we won't see that we are sick?

It's never pleasant to take a good, honest look in the mirror with our emotional defenses let down and all our spiritual pretenses stripped off. But that's the only way we can bring our need before Jesus and learn to walk again. It's the only path from death to life. Take a moment to reread, in another version, Christ's parable of the Pharisee and the tax gatherer . . . and take His message to heart.

> Then [Jesus] gave this illustration to certain people who were confident of their own goodness and looked down on others:
> "Two men went up to the Temple to pray, one was a Pharisee, the other was a tax-collector. The Pharisee stood and prayed like this with himself, 'O God, I do thank thee that I am not like the rest of mankind, greedy, dishonest, impure, or even like that tax-collector over there. I fast twice every week; I give away a tenth-part of all my income.' But the tax-collector stood in a distant corner, scarcely daring to look up to Heaven, and with a gesture of despair, said, 'God, have mercy on a sinner like me.' I assure you that he was the man who went home justified in God's sight, rather than the other one. For everyone who sets himself up as somebody will become a nobody, and the man who makes himself nobody will become somebody." (Luke 18:9–14 PHILLIPS)

77

Chapter 11

The Claims of the Christ

John 5:17–30

In the early 1950s, Boris Nicholayevich Kornfeld, a Jewish medical doctor, was sentenced to a Russian concentration camp, ostensibly for some minor political crime. Because of his training, Kornfeld became a prison surgeon, operating on both fellow prisoners and hated guards in poorly lit, unsanitary conditions. Stripped of his possessions and dignity, as well as his faith in the political system, Kornfeld was led to Jesus by a kind, educated inmate. For the first time, he saw that salvation was not through communism but through Christ.

In that dank, catacomb existence, the seed of faith planted by that one prisoner began to germinate and spread its roots deep into Kornfeld's soul. The doctor could no longer ignore the corruption that filled the prison—the suffering, violence, thefts, and lies. For him, faith was not a wall plaque or bumper sticker; it was a life-changing commitment to the Savior who came to alleviate suffering and rectify injustice. Because he no longer cooperated with their dishonest schemes, Kornfeld increasingly angered those in charge.

The conflict came to a head the day Kornfeld turned in an orderly caught stealing bread from patients dying of malnutrition. His superiors smiled secretly, for they knew that anyone who dared snitch on another inmate would not live long.

At the same time, Kornfeld was assigned a new patient—a young man with sorrowful, empty eyes and a childlike expression. As Kornfeld cared for this man after he came out of surgery, he talked about his new freedom in Christ. Although the man drifted in and out of the anesthesia's influence, the doctor's zeal caught his attention. The patient knew he was hearing about an incredible transformation, and he hung onto the doctor's every word until, at last, he fell asleep.

The next morning the patient was wakened by the sound of running feet and loud noises. In hushed whispers, another patient told him that someone had crept up on the sleeping doctor and crushed his head with eight blows from a plasterer's mallet. The "stoolie" had been silenced.

But Kornfeld's testimony lived on. And it forever changed the life of that one young man with the sorrowful eyes. He survived his illness and the concentration camp and lived to tell the world what he had learned there.

The patient? Aleksandr Solzhenitsyn.[1]

Kornfeld and Solzhenitsyn learned a lesson we can apply today—the claims of Christ were never meant to merely adorn our coat lapels or emblazon our car bumpers. They were meant to make changes in our lives and in the lives of those around us—changes as radical as the claims themselves, which we will examine in our study of John 5.

I. Background

Preceding Christ's remarkable claims was the miraculous healing of a man who had been sick for thirty-eight years (John 5:1–9a). But the Jews' reactions scandalized this merciful act because it took place on the Sabbath (vv. 9b–17). In His response, Jesus claims equality with the Father and incurs a whirlwind of religious wrath.

II. Discourse

In the calm eye of this gathering storm of criticism and treachery, Jesus begins a discourse that is life-changing in its implications.

A. General answer (vv. 17–18). Replying to the Pharisees' accusations, Jesus makes some amazing claims, the first of which is general in nature.

"My Father is working until now, and I Myself am working." (v. 17)

As the following verse reveals, this claim sets in motion a backlash of resistance.

For this cause therefore the Jews were seeking all the more to kill Him, because He not only was breaking the Sabbath, but also was calling God His own Father, making Himself equal with God. (v. 18)

B. Specific claims (vv. 19–30). Moving from the general to the specific, Jesus' claims become not only more profound but more pointed as well.

1. **"I am equal with God"** (vv. 19–20). Throughout the passage, Jesus never refers to God generically as *our* Father. It is always *My* Father or *the* Father (see vv. 17, 19). In doing so, He claims a unique relationship with God. The Jews recognize the implications of the claim: that in "calling God His own Father," Jesus is "making Himself equal with God" (v. 18b). And Jesus claims not only an equal relationship with God but also equality in the work they share.

"Truly, truly, I say to you, the Son can do nothing of Himself, unless it is something He sees

1. Story retold from the account in Chuck Colson's *Loving God* (Grand Rapids, Mich.: Zondervan Publishing House, 1983), pp. 27–34.

the Father doing; for whatever the Father does, these things the Son also does in like manner. For the Father loves the Son, and shows Him all things that He Himself is doing; and greater works than these will He show Him, that you may marvel." (vv. 19–20)

Like a shadow, which is neither identical to nor independent of the substance from which it is cast, so the Son and the Father are distinct from, yet dependent upon, each other.

2. **"I am the giver of life"** (vv. 21, 26). An example of the "greater works" in verse 20 is given in verses 21 and 26.

"For just as the Father raises the dead and gives them life, even so the Son also gives life to whom He wishes. . . . For just as the Father has life in Himself, even so He gave to the Son also to have life in Himself."

To assert His equality, Jesus claims to have the same power the Father does over the dead. This statement comes from the germinal seed of truth buried in John's prologue, stating that "in Him was life" (1:4). It finds its fruition in the raising of Lazarus in chapter 11. While many may claim the power to heal, no one but Christ claims the ability to raise the dead.

The Gift of Life

Man can give medicine when sickness comes,
food when hunger comes,
help when weakness comes,
love when loneliness comes.
But when death comes, man can give
only sympathy,
only compassion,
Never the gift of life.
Only God can do that.

---

3. **"I am the final judge"** (5:22–23). Jesus next delivers perhaps His most striking claim thus far:

"For not even the Father judges anyone, but He has given all judgment to the Son." (v. 22)

Most people mistakenly believe that God the Father is the final judge of humankind. But this verse, along with many others in the New Testament, indicates that Jesus will be the judge (see Acts 10:42; 2 Cor. 5:10; 2 Tim. 4:1). And just as a judge is esteemed as Your Honor, and all participants rise when he enters the courtroom, so it is only fitting that the highest judge, enthroned at the right hand of God the Father, should receive such honor from His subjects.

Honoring the Judge

We stand in the presence of a judge who was once a prisoner Himself—slanderously accused, unjustly tried, brutally beaten, mocked by His executioners, and killed on a cross.

Because the Father honored Christ's selfless sacrifice—truly innocent, dying without speaking a word in His own defense—we, too, should reverently and publicly honor the Lord Jesus.

Therefore also God highly exalted Him, and bestowed on Him the name which is above every name, that at the name of Jesus every knee should bow, of those who are in heaven, and on earth, and under the earth, and that every tongue should confess that Jesus Christ is Lord, to the glory of God the Father. (Phil. 2:9–11)

---

4. **"I determine everyone's destiny"** (John 5:24). Not only does Jesus claim to be the judge, He claims to be the ticket out of the courtroom for any who stand guilty.

   "Truly, truly, I say to you, he who hears My word, and believes Him who sent Me, has eternal life, and does not come into judgment, but has passed out of death into life." (v. 24)

   The words "truly, truly" ring out like a town crier's "hear ye, hear ye," drawing attention to this important message. It is important because it carries good news: eternal life without the threat of judgment. But first, two things are required: a hearing ear and a believing heart. Anyone who accepts this gift by faith buries forever the fear of eternal separation from God (see Rom. 8:1, 38–39).

5. **"I will raise the dead"** (John 5:25–29). In another dramatic "hear ye, hear ye" announcement, Jesus gives us some of the Bible's clearest information regarding resurrection.

> "Truly, truly, I say to you, an hour is coming
> and now is, when the dead shall hear the voice
> of the Son of God; and those who hear shall
> live. For just as the Father has life in Himself,
> even so He gave to the Son also to have life
> in Himself; and He gave Him authority to exe-
> cute judgment, because He is the Son of Man.
> Do not marvel at this; for an hour is coming,
> in which all who are in the tombs shall hear
> His voice, and shall come forth; those who did
> the good deeds to a resurrection of life, those
> who committed the evil deeds to a resurrec-
> tion of judgment." (vv. 25–29)

Three crystal-clear facts surface regarding the final judgment: (1) there will definitely be life after death; (2) every
person will be affected by it; and (3) humanity will fall
into two, and only two, categories. Though these facts
shine through, some have found verse 29 a little confus-
ing. Taken by itself, it seems to indicate that eternal destiny is based on our deeds—good or evil—rather than
on belief or unbelief. But as we study John's writings, it's
clear that he saw "doing good" as a natural outgrowth of
the saving gospel's seed planted in the heart of the believer at the time of the new birth. As he wrote in his
third letter,

> Beloved, do not imitate what is evil, but what
> is good. The one who does good is of God; the
> one who does evil has not seen God. (3 John 11;
> see also 1 John 2:29; 3:10; 4:7–11)

From the viewpoint of the Gospel writers, the "good" life
emerges through a relationship with Christ, and the "evil"
life encroaches through separation from Him (compare
Matt. 25:31–46).

6. **"I am always doing the will of God"** (John 5:30). As a
shadow does not move on its own initiative, so Jesus
moves only in cadence with the Father's footsteps.

> "I can do nothing on My own initiative. As
> I hear, I judge; and My judgment is just, be-
> cause I do not seek My own will, but the will
> of Him who sent Me."

This verse finds an echo in chapter 8.

> Jesus therefore said, "When you lift up the Son
> of Man, then you will know that I am He, and
> I do nothing on My own initiative, but I speak

these things as the Father taught Me. And He who sent Me is with Me; He has not left Me alone, for I always do the things that are pleasing to Him." (vv. 28–29)

Taking to Heart the Claims of Christ

The claims of Christ are so radical that they cry out for an equally radical commitment to Him.

The nameless prisoner who shared the claims of Christ with Dr. Boris Kornfeld made such a commitment.

For Kornfeld, too, the revolutionary claims of Christ, which stood in sharp relief against the moral bankruptcy of communism, elicited such a commitment.

And in the frightened young Solzhenitsyn, whose life teetered between heaven and hell in a prison hospital ward, there developed such a commitment.

How about you? Have Christ's radical claims made any radical changes in your life?

Living Insights

Let's take a moment to re-anchor ourselves in the context of Jesus' claims in John 5. Jesus had come to Jerusalem to honor God the Father by celebrating one of His feasts. Just north of the temple, near the Sheep Gate, was the pool of Bethesda, around which was a collection of the most miserable, hurting, hopeless people one could imagine. Many of us can barely look at pictures of sick and suffering people let alone personally walk among them. But Jesus stopped here first. He did not shrink away but went right up to a man who had been waiting for healing by that pool for thirty-eight years.

After asking this man if he wanted to get well and patiently listening to his answer, Jesus instantly freed him from the captivity of his frail body. "Get up!" was Jesus' liberating command, and then He sent strength surging through limbs weakened for a lifetime, saying, "Pick up your mat and walk" (v. 8 NIV).

How long had it been since this man walked? Had he *ever* walked? A minute ago, he couldn't even get himself into the pool, and now he could not only walk but carry his bed! What a great occasion for joy! What a great occasion to celebrate God's mercy and healing!

Unless one is a legalist.

Legalists don't see people; they only see what rules others might be breaking. Legalists don't celebrate God's mercy; they're too busy pronouncing their own judgments. Legalists don't take joy in life; they wind up killing the spirit, and sometimes, as in Jesus' case, they seek to literally kill the one who opposes their rules and expectations (John 5:18).

In contrast, Jesus, the giver of life and healing, sought to be about His Father's work, even on the Sabbath. What do you think God meant us to rest from when He instituted the Sabbath, and what do you think His continuing work is (see Isa. 58:13–14 compared with Matt. 6:24; see also Matt. 12:7–14)?

_____

_____

_____

_____

_____

_____

_____

Were the Pharisees highly moral people (compare Mark 7:14–23)? Can morality give a person life? Why are people mistaken about this so easily?

_____

_____

_____

_____

_____

_____

Who has the right to judge another person (John 5:22, 27)?

_____

Legalism is really a system of judging and condemning others while seeking honor for ourselves, isn't it? Take a moment to remind yourself of what Jesus and His servants taught about judging others.

Matthew 7:1–2 _____

_____

_____

Luke 6:37 _____

_____

_____

John 7:24 _____

_____

_____

Romans 14 _____

_____

_____

_____

James 4:12 _____

_____

_____

Life is found in the Person of Jesus Christ, not in any system of rule-keeping, no matter how biblically based it may be. And our Lord is so good, isn't He? He sees *us*, not His own checklist of rights and wrongs, and He takes the initiative to meet us in our need. At His word we can be healed—even of a lifelong, crippling spirit of judgmentalism.

Ask Jesus if judging and criticizing others is a problem for you, and if He reveals that it is, humbly take it to Him for healing, won't you? Freedom will be yours, just as it was for the man by the pool—and not only yours, but all the people your life touches.

Chapter 12

Witnesses for the Defense
John 5:31–47

Mark Lane was an attorney who defended a dead man—and got results.

His client? Lee Harvey Oswald, accused assassin of President John F. Kennedy. But before Lane could even begin preparing his defense, Oswald, too, was shot and killed. Another attorney might have closed the case, but not Mark Lane. In fact, he worked harder than ever to prove that his deceased client had not acted alone in the presidential assassination plot.

Lane documented his findings in the best-selling book *Rush to Judgment*. The facts, interviews, and pictures he gathered cast a convincing shadow of doubt over the single-assassin theory. So influential was the book that public opinion shifted, causing 69 percent of the people polled to disagree with the accepted view that a lone assassin was responsible for the president's death.

Why was the single-assassin theory questioned? How was the public swayed? Through the use of key witnesses.

In a similar manner, Jesus marshaled key witnesses to His defense when the Pharisees accused Him of being a Sabbath breaker and a blasphemer.

I. Bearing Witness: The Law
The fifth chapter of John's Gospel provides us with a drama in three vignettes. First, a *miracle*, where a man paralyzed for thirty-eight years is instantly healed. Second, a *series of claims*, where Jesus Christ testifies that He is the Son of God. Third, a *defense*, where five witnesses are introduced to verify His claims. To begin His defense, Jesus makes a startling statement.

"If I alone bear witness of Myself, My testimony is not true." (v. 31)

A. Meaning of the statement. Jesus does not mean that His claims are false, only that His testimony alone would not be valid in a court of law. According to rabbinic sayings and Jewish procedure, "none may be believed when he testifies of himself."[1]

---

1. Leon Morris, *The Gospel according to John,* rev. ed., The New International Commentary on the New Testament Series (Grand Rapids, Mich.: William B. Eerdmans Publishing Co., 1995), p. 287, fn. 92.

B. Reason for the statement. According to Jewish law, even a single witness was insufficient to determine the truth of a matter.

> "A single witness shall not rise up against a man on account of any iniquity or any sin which he has committed; on the evidence of two or three witnesses a matter shall be confirmed." (Deut. 19:15)

II. Hearing the Witnesses: Their Testimonies

In John 5:32–47, the Lord appeals to five witnesses in His defense. Imagine yourself as a juror and Jesus on trial as the defendant. The first witness is called.

A. Witness number one: God the Father.

> "There is another who bears witness of Me, and I know that the testimony which He bears of Me is true." (v. 32)

Two grammatical points in the original Greek add color to this verse. To begin with, notice how Jesus introduces the Father: "There is another." The word *another* in the Greek may mean "another of the same kind."[2] It is probably a subtle reference to deity (compare 14:16, where He uses the same word to describe the Holy Spirit). The second point is that the Greek construction for the verb "bears witness" indicates continual action. The Father continually testifies to the claims of Christ. At Jesus' birth, the Father announced the arrival with prophets, angels, and a miraculous star. At Jesus' baptism, the Father testified: "This is My beloved Son, in whom I am well-pleased" (Matt. 3:17b) and later reaffirmed His own testimony at the Transfiguration (17:5). In a searing rebuke, Jesus underscores the Father's ongoing testimony to His accusers.

> "And the Father who sent Me, He has borne witness of Me. You have neither heard His voice at any time, nor seen His form. And you do not have His word abiding in you, for you do not believe Him whom He sent." (John 5:37–38)

B. Witness number two: John the forerunner. Jesus next calls John the Baptist to the witness stand.

---

2. The Greek word is *allos*. Leon Morris tells us, "Many commentators maintain that [*allos*] denotes 'another of the same kind,' [while its cousin *heteros* means] 'another of a different kind.' . . . If this distinction holds the meaning, here will be '"*another of the same kind as myself*" . . . by which the evangelist suggests Christ's unique unity with the Father' (Edwin A. Abbott, *Johannine Grammar* [London, 1906], p. 2730). But many writers do not observe the distinction, and, as John employs *heteros* once only (in 19:37), we do not have enough information to be sure that he did." Morris, *The Gospel according to John,* p. 288, fn. 96. The best supports for Jesus' unity with the Father are His own direct statements, such as "I and the Father are one" (John 10:30; see also John 17:21–23).

"You have sent to John, and he has borne witness to the truth. But the witness which I receive is not from man, but I say these things that you may be saved. He was the lamp that was burning and was shining and you were willing to rejoice for a while in his light." (vv. 33–35)

John the Baptist's testimony was clear and simple:

The next day he saw Jesus coming to him, and said, "Behold, the Lamb of God who takes away the sin of the world! This is He on behalf of whom I said, 'After me comes a Man who has a higher rank than I, for He existed before me.' And I did not recognize Him, but in order that He might be manifested to Israel, I came baptizing in water." And John bore witness saying, "I have beheld the Spirit descending as a dove out of heaven, and He remained upon Him. And I did not recognize Him, but He who sent me to baptize in water said to me, 'He upon whom you see the Spirit descending and remaining upon Him, this is the one who baptizes in the Holy Spirit.' And I have seen, and have borne witness that this is the Son of God." (1:29–34)

"For a while" the Jewish leaders were "willing to rejoice" in the light of John's ministry (5:35). Was it because they believed him, repented of their sins, and prepared their hearts for the coming Messiah? Leon Morris thinks otherwise.

It may be that there is an idea of lighthearted merrymaking where there should have been serious purpose. The Jews never did take John seriously. They never came to grips with his message. John was steadily, unflickeringly, pointing the way in his stern call to seriousness of purpose. And these Jews, who professed to be the people of God and to be seeking the way of God, just as steadily ignored his essential message. Instead they took him to be part of the ecclesiastical furniture, so to speak. They exulted in God's gift of a prophet to their generation.[3]

They were honored to have a prophet, but they treated him and the One who sent him with dishonor by not heeding his divinely appointed message.

3. Morris, *The Gospel according to John,* pp. 289–90.

C. Witness number three: Jesus' own works. The defense now moves from verbal to visual evidence. Verse 36 of chapter 5 presents Exhibit A.

"But the witness which I have is greater than that of John; for the works which the Father has given Me to accomplish, the very works that I do, bear witness of Me, that the Father has sent Me."

John's Gospel provides irrefutable evidence for Christ's divinity. He has already turned water into the finest of aged wines, healed a government official's son long-distance, and restored a paralytic. In the pages that follow, He will miraculously feed five thousand, walk on water, heal a blind man, and raise Lazarus from the dead. Jesus' works speak for themselves, yet the defense doesn't rest. Instead, Jesus calls forth another witness.

D. Witness number four: the Scriptures.

"You search the Scriptures, because you think that in them you have eternal life; and it is these that bear witness of Me; and you are unwilling to come to Me, that you may have life. I do not receive glory from men; but I know you, that you do not have the love of God in yourselves. I have come in My Father's name, and you do not receive Me; if another shall come in his own name, you will receive him. How can you believe, when you receive glory from one another, and you do not seek the glory that is from the one and only God?" (vv. 39–44)

These rigid literalists couldn't see the Messiah because God's Word was not truly abiding in them and God's Son was not the object of their faith. The Old Testament Scriptures megaphoned news of the coming Messiah (see Luke 24:27, 44; Acts 8:30–35). But these Jews turned a deaf ear (Luke 13:34).[4]

---

4. "After the destruction of the temple of Solomon in 586 B.C., the Jewish scholars of the Exile substituted the study of the Law for the observance of the temple ritual and sacrifices. They pored over the OT, endeavoring to extract the fullest possible meaning from its words, because they believed that the very study itself would bring them life. By so doing they missed the chief subject of the OT revelation. Jesus claimed the Law, the Prophets, and the Psalms (Writings) as witnesses to his person and claims (Luke 24:44). He rebuked his hearers for their inconsistency in studying the Scriptures so diligently while rejecting his claims, which were founded on those same Scriptures." Merrill C. Tenney, "The Gospel of John," *The Expositor's Bible Commentary*, gen. ed. Frank E. Gaebelein (Grand Rapids, Mich.: Zondervan Publishing House, 1981), vol. 9, p. 68.

> ### Some Personal Application
>
> It's easy to skate on the cold, impersonal outer sur-faces of life—to get caught up in the technical, the pe-ripheral, the superficial.
>
> For a lawyer trafficking in the legal maze, it's easy to become enamored with the intricacies of the law and yet never develop a heart for justice.
>
> For a doctor, it's easy to become swept up in the swirl of state-of-the-art medicine and never develop a heart of compassion.
>
> For the professional minister or the serious student of the Scriptures, it's easy to become enraptured with exegesis instead of Jesus, carrying on a love affair with the printed page rather than with the person of Christ.
>
> The Bible was given not simply as a legal document or a self-help book but as a love letter. And if that letter doesn't draw us irresistibly toward Christ, then it's pos-sible that we, like those prosecutorial Jews, do not have His Word abiding in us.

E. Witness number five: Moses. Jesus now turns the courtroom tables and points an indicting finger at His litigious accusers.

> "Do not think that I will accuse you before the Fa-ther; the one who accuses you is Moses, in whom you have set your hope. For if you believed Moses, you would believe Me; for he wrote of Me. But if you do not believe his writings, how will you believe My words?" (John 5:45–47)

As His trump card, Jesus pulls an ace out of the deck of Jewish heroes: Moses. Why Moses? Because, like Abraham, Isaac, and Jacob, Moses was one of the founding fathers of Judaism. He spearheaded the Exodus, delivered God's Law to the people, and was looked up to with reverence. But when did Moses ever write of Christ? Turn back to the prophetic pages of Deuteronomy 18.

> "The Lord your God will raise up for you a prophet like me from among you, from your countrymen, you shall listen to him. . . . 'And it shall come about that whoever will not listen to My words which he shall speak in My name, I Myself will re-quire it of him.'" (vv. 15, 19)

But how can we be sure Jesus was the prophet referred to by

Moses? Read Peter's words in Acts 3. Notice that he quotes the passage from Deuteronomy.

> "But the things which God announced beforehand by the mouth of all the prophets, that His Christ should suffer, He has thus fulfilled. Repent therefore and return, that your sins may be wiped away, in order that times of refreshing may come from the presence of the Lord; and that He may send Jesus, the Christ appointed for you, whom heaven must receive until the period of restoration of all things about which God spoke by the mouth of His holy prophets from ancient time. Moses said, 'The Lord God shall raise up for you a prophet like me from your brethren; to Him you shall give heed in everything He says to you. And it shall be that every soul that does not heed that prophet shall be utterly destroyed from among the people.'" (vv. 18–23)

III. The Verdict: A Serious Choice

The witnesses have been carefully chosen. Each has taken the stand. The evidence has been judiciously presented. The defense rests. As a member of the jury, you must deliberate. You must weigh the evidence. It's a sobering decision, for the verdict you reach about Christ is a serious one. It is, quite literally, a matter of life or death—*your* life or death.

Living Insights

"You diligently study the Scriptures because you think that by them you possess eternal life" (John 5:39 NIV). These words of Jesus are every bit as relevant today as they were when He first spoke them, aren't they?

Do you ever get the feeling that many of us Christians today are more interested in becoming Bible students rather than disciples of Christ? We wind up studying the road but never following it to Christ. We underline it, memorize it, paraphrase it, and quote it at people. We take its words apart and put them back together again. We say, "The Bible saves!" But it's really not the Bible that saves; it is Jesus Christ who saves.

It is Jesus who atones for our sins, Jesus who forgives us, Jesus who gives us eternal life, Jesus who guides us by grace. If we miss Him, as the Jewish scholars did in Jesus' days on earth, we miss the whole message of His Book. We miss the forest for the trees. We miss the whole sweep of salvation history for a few scattered practical applications.

Now, don't get us wrong, we're not saying to toss your Bible aside and somehow mystically commune with Christ. His Word is the way we come to know Him. His Word reveals His heart, His plan, His design for living. In His Word He explains how we can have a relationship with Him, so it is essential that we do study and know it.

What we always need to remember, though, is that His Book is not an end in itself. Our study of the Scriptures should always point us toward Christ. Donald Grey Barnhouse explains with an illustration.

> Suppose somebody were staying in an Atlantic city hotel and his room had a window overlooking a beautiful view of the Atlantic Ocean. Wouldn't you think something was wrong if they came to you and said, "Now I want to tell you all about the window in my room. This window has eight glass panes on one side and eight on the other side. It's a casement window which measures so many inches by so many inches. I want to take scratchings of the glass to give you a chemical analysis of my window." Someone who said that would be missing the whole point of having a window. The window is there so you can see the ocean; not so you can study the window.
>
> Well, the Bible is a window. The purpose of the Bible is that you may look through it and see Jesus Christ. Some people stop with the Bible. I will yield to no man in my belief in the Bible, in its divine origin, in the fact that it is divine, verbally inspired revelation. But I say that the Bible is not a thing to be analyzed, criticized, outlined and examined, just for its own sake. That would be just like sitting in a room and writing a book about a window, without seeing the ocean with its waves curling up the beach or the way the lights and clouds play upon the water. . . . The window allows us to see the beauty which lies beyond. The Bible is the way to life in Jesus Christ.[5]

As we continue our study in the Gospel of John in the next volume, *Following Christ . . . The Man of God,* be careful not to lose Christ in the midst of the Greek and Hebrew words, the parallel passages, the errors of the Pharisees, and the personal applications. Remember that *Jesus is the point* of all the Scripture, so keep your eyes focused on Him and your ears attuned to Him.

5. Donald Grey Barnhouse, *The Love Life* (Glendale, Calif.: Gospel Light Publications, Regal Books, 1973), pp. 72–73.

⬛ *Digging Deeper*

As you study all of God's Word, here's a key to help you recognize Jesus in each book of the Bible.

In the Book of . . .	**He is . . .**
Genesis	The woman's Seed
Exodus	The Passover Lamb
Leviticus	The atoning Sacrifice
Numbers	The bronze Serpent
Deuteronomy	The promised Prophet
Joshua	The Captain of the Hosts
Judges	My Deliverer
Ruth	My heavenly Kinsman
1 and 2 Samuel, 1 and 2 Kings 1 and 2 Chronicles	The promised King
Ezra and Nehemiah	The Restorer of the nation
Esther	My Advocate
Job	My Redeemer
Psalms	My All in All
Proverbs	My Pattern
Ecclesiastes	My Goal
Song of Solomon	My Beloved
The Prophets	The coming Prince of Peace
Matthew	Christ the King
Mark	Christ the Suffering Servant
Luke	Christ the Son of Man
John	Christ the Son of God
Acts	Risen, seated, and sending
The Epistles	Indwelling and filling
Revelation	Returning and reigning[6]

---

6. Adapted from *Illustrating Great Words of the New Testament,* by J. B. Fowler Jr. (Nashville, Tenn.: Broadman Press, 1991), p. 98.

Books for Probing Further

"In the beginning was the Word, and the Word was with God, and the Word was God. . . . And the Word became flesh, and dwelt among us, and we beheld His glory, glory as of the only begotten from the Father, full of grace and truth" (John 1:1, 14).

Deity was never so awesome
As when it nursed from a young maiden's breast.
No pomp. No pageantry.
No flash. No fanfare.
God slipped unpretentiously into the warm lake of humanity,
With barely a ripple of notice.
In His wake
A quiet greatness
Moved in concentric circles,
Touching everyone He met:
    a fisherman, weathered and worn;
    a woman, Samaritan and shameful;
    a man, thirty-eight years lame.
A rolled-up pallet,
An empty water pot,
Nets hung out to dry,
Forever left behind
    for Him,
        who was full of grace and truth;
    for Him,
        whose brimming glory
        spilled into their empty lives.
Where there was meaningless labor,
    He gave mission.
Where there was thirst for forgiveness,
    He gave living water.
Where there was hurt,
    He gave healing.
Deity was never so winsome
As when the Light of the World
    touched these dimly burning wicks,
    and gave them a reason to shine.

—Ken Gire

We hope these first studies in John have helped *your* light shine a little brighter and a little warmer for Christ and that His winsome ways will fan the flame of your spiritual passion. To further feed that fire, we recommend the following books.

I. Jesus Christ

Clowney, Edmund P. *The Unfolding Mystery: Discovering Christ in the Old Testament.* Colorado Springs, Colo.: NavPress, 1988.

Neill, Stephen. *The Supremacy of Jesus.* The Jesus Library Series. Downers Grove, Ill.: InterVarsity Press, 1984.

Sproul, R. C. *The Glory of Christ.* Wheaton, Ill.: Tyndale House Publishers, 1990.

Yancey, Philip. *The Jesus I Never Knew.* Grand Rapids, Mich.: Zondervan Publishing House, 1995.

II. Commentaries

Barclay, William. *The Gospel of John.* Vol. 1. Rev. ed. The Daily Study Bible Series. Philadelphia, Pa.: Westminster Press, 1975.

Barnhouse, Donald Grey. *The Love Life.* Glendale, Calif.: Gospel Light Publications, Regal Books, 1973.

Carson, D. A. *The Gospel according to John.* Grand Rapids, Mich.: William B. Eerdmans Publishing Co., 1991.

Milne, Bruce. *The Message of John: Here Is Your King!* The Bible Speaks Today Series. Downers Grove, Ill.: InterVarsity Press, 1993.

Morris, Leon. *The Gospel according to John.* Rev. ed. The New International Commentary on the New Testament Series. Grand Rapids, Mich.: William B. Eerdmans Publishing Co., 1995.

Tenney, Merrill C. *John: The Gospel of Belief.* 1976. Reprint, Grand Rapids, Mich.: William B. Eerdmans Publishing Co., 1989.

III. Grace and Legalism

Bridges, Jerry. *Transforming Grace: Living Confidently in God's Unfailing Love.* Colorado Springs, Colo.: NavPress, 1991.

Hall, Dudley. *Grace Works: Letting God Rescue You from Empty Religion.* Ann Arbor, Mich.: Servant Publications, Vine Books, 1992.

Manning, Brennan. *The Ragamuffin Gospel: Good News for the Bedraggled, Beat-Up, and Burnt Out.* Portland, Ore.: Multnomah Press, 1990.

Miller, David R. *Breaking Free: Rescuing Families from the Clutches of Legalism.* Grand Rapids, Mich.: Baker Book House, 1992.

Smedes, Lewis B. *Shame and Grace: Healing the Shame We Don't Deserve.* San Francisco, Calif.: HarperSanFrancisco, 1993.

Swindoll, Charles R. *The Grace Awakening.* Dallas, Tex.: Word Publishing, 1990.

VanVonderen, Jeff. *Tired of Trying to Measure Up.* Minneapolis, Minn.: Bethany House Publishers, 1989.

Yancey, Philip. *What's So Amazing about Grace?* Grand Rapids, Mich.: Zondervan Publishing House, 1997.

Some of these books may be out of print and available only through a library. For those currently available, please contact your local Christian bookstore. Books by Charles R. Swindoll, as well as some books by other authors, may be obtained through Insight for Living.

Insight for Living also offers study guides on many books of the Bible, as well as on a variety of issues and biblical personalities. For more information, see the ordering instructions that follow and contact the office that serves you.

Notes

Notes

Ordering Information

Beholding Christ . . . The Son of God

If you would like to order additional study guides, purchase the cassette series that accompanies this guide, or request our product catalogs, please contact the office that serves you.

United States and International locations:

Insight for Living
Post Office Box 69000
Anaheim, CA 92817-0900
1-800-772-8888, 24 hours a day, seven days a week
(714) 575-5000, 8:00 A.M. to 4:30 P.M., Pacific time,
Monday to Friday

Canada:

Insight for Living Ministries
Post Office Box 2510
Vancouver, BC, Canada V6B 3W7
1-800-663-7639, 24 hours a day, seven days a week

Australia:

Insight for Living, Inc.
20 Albert Street
Blackburn, VIC 3130, Australia
Toll-free 1800-772-888 or (03) 9877-4277, 8:30 A.M. to 5:00 P.M.,
Monday to Friday

World Wide Web:

www.insight.org

Study Guide Subscription Program

Study guide subscriptions are available. Please call or write the office nearest you to find out how you can receive our study guides on a regular basis.